Macramé for Beginners

The Complete Step-by-Step Guide to Mastering Macrame

Discover Secret Macrame Tips & Make Your First Macrame Project

Includes Projects for Kids, Teens & Pet Accessories

By

Sophia Knott

Contents

Introduction

Do you feel ready to explore the fascinating world of Macrame? Whether you've never tied a knot or have dabbled in a few, "Macrame for Beginners" is the best manual to teach you how to master this lovely technique. This book is intended to empower and encourage you on your macrame adventure, from learning the techniques to making your first item. We will take you by the hand and walk you through each step of the macrame process in this detailed guide. The prerequisites are a willingness to learn and a love for producing stunning, handcrafted items. No prior experience or specific skills are needed. You'll be stunned at how far your macrame talents have come by the time you finish this book. Beginning with a detailed introduction to the craft of Macrame, "Macrame for Beginners" explores its rich history and wide range of uses. You'll learn about the appeal of Macrame and how it has become a cutting-edge craft that combines tradition and modern design. Before starting, learn about the necessary equipment and supplies, such as cords, beads, and embellishments. After laying the groundwork, we'll move on to the knots, the core of Macrame. You will learn how to tie some of the most important knots in Macrame, including the square knot, spiral knot, and half hitch. You'll soon understand each knot's technique thanks to the clear, step-by-step directions and accompanying drawings, developing your confidence and skills as you go. As you read the book, you'll find a selection of hand-picked projects for beginners. You can easily reproduce any project because it comes with detailed, simple-to-follow directions and attractive illustrations. These projects, which range from wall hangings to plant hangers, bracelets, and keychains, highlight your newly gained macrame skills and give you a sense of success.

However, "Macrame for Beginners" teaches you more than simply the knots and tasks. To help you avoid typical problems and make your designs truly shine, we've provided exclusive advice from skilled macrame craftsmen. Learn how to select the proper cable thickness, design distinctive patterns, use assorted color schemes, and insert personalized touches to make your macrame items stand out.

As you delve deeper into the realm of Macrame, you'll discover that it provides a creative outlet and a calming and contemplative experience. You can calm down, unwind, and discover delight in the present moment by engaging in the rhythmic act of knotting. Macrame is more than just making attractive objects; it's also about nurturing your spirit and learning to practice mindfulness.

Therefore, "Macrame for Beginners" is your definitive guide to learning Macrame, whether you're looking for a new hobby, a method to relax, or a way to express your creativity. This book will let you produce magnificent macrame items and realize your artistic potential with thorough instructions, motivational tasks, and insider hints. Prepare yourself for a journey of knotting, exploration, and self-expression. Let's start your macrame journey right away!

Chapter 1: Knots & Techniques

An elaborate, colorful design uses hand-timed knots in the flexible, historical textile technique called macramé. Simple materials like hemp, jute, leather, yarn, or cotton thread may be used as the macramé cord. In the current day, the art was resurrected to produce elegant home furnishings. Macrame work gives up various creation options and may be adorned with wooden and glass beads, colored threads, and other embellishments.

Uses

- To create jewelry, wall hangings, window treatments, key chains, and plant hangers

- for use in creating placemats, bikinis, bell-fringed curtains, hammocks, belts, friendship bracelets, and curtains.

- to adorn objects like lamp bases, flowerpots, bottles, purses, picture frames, and knife handles

1.1: Materials and tools needed

Macrame cord. A macrame cord is the first and most important item you will need. Macrame cords come in various thicknesses, colors, and styles. The sale of macrame cords is widely available both online and offline. A 3mm–4mm single-strand linen macrame cord is ideal for novices since it is flexible, simple to knot, and easy to unravel if you make a mistake.

See our instructions if you need assistance with the fundamental macrame knots. Make sure to review the project requirements before selecting your cord. Compared to a smaller craft like a macrame bracelet, you'll need a significantly thicker string if you're building a huge structure, such as a chair or hammock.

Steel S hooks. The benefit of metal S hooks is that you may hang your item while working on it. Tying tidy, well-organized knots may be challenging if your item is lying down. Working on a large project is simpler if you also have S hooks. They are inexpensive, and you could already have some in your house!

Wooden hoops. You'll need hooks and beads to hang macrame items like this crochet plant or add ornamental components (as in our crochet belt). You may purchase hoops or beads made of metal, plastic, glass, or wood. They are simple to paint to match your project or leave unpainted for a more rustic appearance.

Wooden dowels. If you intend to create wall hangings, a wood dowel is needed. They provide a solid foundation for you to begin knotting your project. Thanks to the beads on the ends of the dowels, your product won't slide off the edges. You can additionally utilize a tree limb for a more natural appearance.

Dependable macramé scissors. For Macrame, a good set of scissors is necessary. They are particularly handy for tidying up the ends of your rope, so they look like this macrame bird keychain.

Measuring tape. This one is really simple, and chances are you already have one if you like crafting or doing a bit of DIY! You'll need a measuring tape to verify that the lengths of macrame thread you cut are all the same size.

Metal brush or comb. You must brush out the macrame cord tails to separate them. For this, a metal brush performs well; we believe a pet brush performs especially well. A little brush with stainless steel bristles to separate the strings and a smooth hardwood handle for a secure grasp will be ideal for your macrame requirements.

Macrame board made of wood. A wooden board is useful for making little macrame products, like jewelry or keychains. As you tie or bead your strings, the board's slots along the edge will hold them for you. It may also be placed on your lap and is a terrific method to guarantee that you have a stable, level surface.

Macrame basket for storing. Your macrame supplies may be kept in a sweet basket, which fits the rustic aesthetic of this craft. It would look wonderful tucked up in a cozy living room nook. The amount of macrame materials you have will determine the kind of basket you require. We advise these wonderful wicker baskets that come in a package of four for individuals with a little or medium kit.

1.2: Step-by-step instructions for the basic knots

Conditions Specific to Macrame

Here are a few phrases that are often used in the directions for most macramé projects before you start:

- Cord knotting. This is the string or group of cords used to tie the knot in a particular stitch.

- A cord with a knot. This is the rope or group of cords around which the knotting cords wrap. Although the knotting or knot-bearing cord may vary from one project stage to the next, the pattern will let you know.

- Sennit. This describes a group of single stitch that is stitched repeatedly. You have a stitch of 6 half knots; for instance, if you knit 6 half-knot threads in a row.

1: Half Knot

A sinnet is often made using half knots (note the specific word!). A natural spiral produced by a series of Half Knots is often utilized in plant hanger designs. Four cords are used while working the Half Knot. The two core cords support the knots, while the two outside cords serve as the knotting cords.

1. Cross both knot-bearing cords with the left tying cord beneath the right one.

2. Pass the right knotting cord over the left knotting cord and the two knot-bearing cords.

3. Tighten the knot by pulling on the ropes.

2: Square Knot

The Half Knot is continued in the Square Knot. (The "half" is "half of the square"). So, you tie the first section of the knot exactly like a half-knot, and then you tie another half-tie using the opposing strands to complete the square.

1. Perform steps 1-3 to complete the Half Knot as described above.

2. Pass the left binding cord beneath the right tying cord and over both knot-bearing cords.

3. Pass the left knotting cord over the opposite knotting cord and beneath the two knot-bearing cords.

4. To secure knotting cords, pull them.

3: Half Hitch Knots

For various effects, it may be worked horizontally, vertically, diagonally, and with a variety of knotting cords or knot-bearing cords. Half Hitch Knots may also be tied from the right to the left or left to the right. This knot is one of the more popular macrame knots because it is simple and adaptable.

4: Two-Half Hitch

Two half-hitch hooks are done one after another to form a double half-hitch knot. The term "Clove Hitch" has been used to describe this. Repeating the knotting processes twice may make any of the below-listed Half Hitch knot variants into a double half-hitch.

5: (Left to Right) Horizontal Half Hitch

In this illustration, the cord on the far left is the knot-bearer, while the cord on the far right is the tying cord. Different cables have distinct functions depending on the design, but your project instructions should specify which cords do what.

6: Right to Left Half Hitch in Horizontal

Follow the instructions above, using the cord on the right as the knot-bearing thread and the cord on the next row to the left as a knotting car to complete the horizontal half hook from right to left.

7: Diagnostic Half-Hitch Right to Left

The difference between the Vertical Half Hitch and the Vertical Half Hitch is that the cord holding the knot is diagonally when the stitches are made.

8: Right to Left Diagonal Half Hitch

Follow the instructions above, using the cord on the right as the knot-bearing thread and the cord to the left as the knotting cord to complete the double diagonal hitch from right to left.

9: Right to Left Vertical Single Half Hitch

Follow the instructions above, placing the shorter end of the tying cord at the correct spot and the longer one at the left to complete the vertical half hook from right to left.

1.3: Practical examples of using the basic knot

While fancy, decorative, or ornamental knots may not be strong, they can have a pleasing look. They often have intricate structures and repeated patterns. They have been around since the beginning of time when they were employed to emphasize a nautical vessel's ship like design. A decorative knot may be tied with one or more strands and can be used by itself or with other decorative knots of the same kind.

The tying guidelines may be used to create macramé designs, jewelry (necklaces, bracelets), wraps around poles, drapes, handles, and more. They may be fastened with paracord, ribbons, rope ends, braids, lanyards, and other materials.

1: Diamond (lanyard) knot

1. Create a rope ring and wrap the rope around it.

2. Thread some rope through the loop.

3. Take it up.

4. Pass it into the newly created loop.

5. Pass it over the initial loop.

6. Pull both ends to tighten while holding the large loop.

7. Place one end of the second rope through the loop.

8. A knot is created.

Tips

- Be aware that the first stages resemble creating a Carrick curve.

- Variation

- Double diamond knots are more intricate and ornate than double lanyard knots. Two strands are used to make it.

Uses

- on key rings and knife tassels.

- As pulls on zippers.

- In designs for bracelets, rings, pendants, earrings, and necklaces.

- using macramé designs.

2: Half knot

1. Cross the two ends over the support,

2. pass one end below the other,

3. remove it, and

4. tighten the standing components.

Utilizations in macramé designs

- in friendship (spiral) bracelets made of hemp

- making jewelry using a half knot twisted or a sinnet.

- Tying bandana or scarf headbands.

3: Monkey's Fist

1. Wrap the rope end horizontally around your finger three times, then.

2. wrap it twice more.

3. Wrap it three times around the horizontal portion after passing it through the loop.

4. Remove it.

5. Add a ball to give the shape a sphere.

6. Pull to cinch.

7. There are no more knots.

Uses

- In zipper pulls, keyrings, keychains, cobra knots, and lanyards. They seem nautical as a result. You can create a fantastic paracord fob using a square knot, lanyard, and monkey's fist.

- To defend oneself (albeit it is a prohibited weapon in several locations).

- As a rock-climbing anchor, insert it into a hole.

- Survival.

- As a means of closing for paracord bracelets.

- As a bookend, dog toy, curtain tieback, doorstop, drawer pull, bookmark, place card, and table number holder.

- Creating jewelry such as necklaces and earrings.

- Making poi heads of fire.

- Boating.

- To amuse your companion, use a ball gag.

- Heaving.

- A parachute handle that is more robust and long-lasting than the standard handle.

- Thanks to its tactical addition, you can swiftly remove your knife.

- A set of cufflinks.

- Design nautical lights, curtain rods, cushions, and knobs.

- As ornaments, planters, or decorative buttons.

- In wedding decorations and macramé designs.

4: The Carrick Bend

1. Make a basic loop using the blue rope that you have.

2. Put the orange strand through the blue rope's arms.

3. Pass it into the blue loop now, as if it were sewn in.

4. Pull out the rope ends as necessary to make the knot more secure.

Uses

- If correctly placed with long tag ends, big weights are securely fastened.

- Capable of producing climbing nets

- that prevent knots from collapsing on exceptionally long ropes.

- Passable via capstans or winches

1.4: Decorative knots to enhance your projects

1: Lark's Head

Use the Lark's Head Knot to fasten your macramé strands to a ring or dowel.

1. Make a loop by folding one macrame cord in half.

2. Lay the folding cord on the work area with the loop down and the ends up.

3. Position your ring or dowel on the folded cord above the loop.

4. Lift the loop over the ring (or dowel).

5. To tighten, pull the rope ends down after pulling them up and into the loop.

2: Lark's Head Knot in Reverse

The Lark's Head knot, also known as the Cow Hook Knot or Reverse Lark's Head knot, is the Lark's Head knot because it looks from the other side.

Whether to use the Lark's Head knot or the Reverse Lark's Head knot is purely a question of taste since both knots are identical.

1. Split a single macramé rope in two.

2. Lay the folding cord on the work area with the loop facing up and the ends facing down.

3. Position your ring or dowel on the folded cord above the loop.

4. Lower the loop over the ring (or dowel).

5. To tighten, pull the rope ends down after pulling them up and into the loop.

3: Vertical Knot

You have probably tied this knot many times without realizing it had a name. It works well for tying off braid ends or cords for plant hangers.

1. Loop the rope by crossing one end over the other.

2. Bring the cable's top end behind the circle and up through it.

3. Secure the cable by tightening both ends.

4: Grouping Knot

A clean and aesthetically pleasing approach to collecting numerous cords is using a gathering knot, also known as a wrapping knot, and gathering wrap. This type of knot is often tied at the very start or finish of a project for a plant hanger. The knot-bearing cords in a project may be some or all of the cords, and a short piece of cord is utilized as the knotting cord.

1. Fold a loop close to the knotting cord's one end.

2. Position the loop so the shorter end points down and the loop is on the top of the knot-bearing cords.

3. While the loop is still in place, securely wrap the knot-bearing cord's long end around them, wrapping at the bottom up to the required length while keeping the top of the loop visible above the wraps.

4. Insert the knotting cord's end through the loop at the top of the wrap.

5. Pull the knotting cord's bottom end to lower the loop into the wrap.

6. Trim the knotting cord's exposed ends just before wrapping.

1.5: Advanced knots for more complex challenges

1: Triangle knot

Two lark's crest knots on the dowel produce this knot.

1. You grab the two sections of your left lark's head knot using your right hand underneath the two cords from the right knot and make the number "four" with all the cords.

2. The left lark's head knot's two cords behind the right knot form an extended demi-circle. As illustrated in the figure, you carefully pull the loop out of the circle with your dominant hand and grasp the remaining cords with your left hand.

3. Holding the form produced in the previous phase in your left hand, grab the ends of the ropes from the right lark's head knot with your right hand.

4. You insert the ends of both cords from the opposite lark's head knot beneath the snake-shaped formation and through the opening between the two knots closest to the dowel.

5. Pull both ends through the loop from the previous stages.

6. Holding both ends, pull outward.

7. It's OK if the form doesn't appear immediately. Pulling in different areas may reveal the outcome.

8. Success! First triangular knot. Excellent job!

2: Sailor knot

One lark's head knot attached to a dowel starts the sailor's knot.

1. You make a D-shaped circle by laying cables over each other.

2. Form an inverted S with the two cord sections to make another loop.

3. Next, thread the cable ends into the hole.

4. Knot complete. Pull it until it resembles our knot.

3: Josephine's knot

1. First, tie two lark's head knots onto your dowel.

2. Loop the cords with your right lark's head knot, as illustrated. Holding the loop with the opposite hand is easy.

3. Make the loop larger to make the following stages easier. After this, place the left lark's head knot cords under the loop over the two left cords directed down. The left-side wires are the "working cords" for the following stage.

4. Pull the working cord ends between the two lark's head knots.

5. After that, you thread it over the nearest side of the circle you made, as seen in the photo.

6. After looping them over the opening, thread these under the left lark's head knot cords in the identical loop.

7. Thread the cables again above the shape.

8. Your knot is almost done. To achieve a balanced knot, tighten or loosen certain sections as above.

4: Pipa's knot

This guide uses one of the lark's head knot's cords, but you may use both.

1. Create a loop as shown. Pinch the loop end with the other hand to simplify the following steps.

2. Wrap the cord up and over the rest.

3. Make a second tight loop around the cord, pointing down.

4. Make another loop with the same rope.

5. Wrap the working cable over and behind the tightened section of the cord again.

6. Repeat until the string runs out or the knot is the appropriate size.

7. Insert the cable end through the little circle instead of completing the procedures above.

Tighten the knot in certain areas to give it a more finished appearance or leave some gap between the coiled cords for depth.

Chapter 2: Tips and Tricks

Macrame is accomplished by using several pieces of string to create an effect similar to that of rope. Many people prefer the use of a string with just one twist. Compared to other types of yarn, such as those used for crocheting or knitting, macramé yarn is significantly more rigid. In addition, it is frequently crafted distinctly. Tips and tricks make Macrame work easy.

2.1: Tips for Customizing Your Macramé Projects

Macramé yarn is either woven or knotted together, unlike the loose strands of yarn typically used in crochet and knitting. It more closely resembles rope, and in certain instances, it is rope; you can begin a macramé creation with rope if you want to. The appearance of your finished macramé piece is the first consideration when selecting the appropriate yarn. Do you wish to tie a knot in a pendant that can hold a robust plant? Then select a chunkier yarn, possibly one that is ropey or cable. Will you use the macramé technique to create a bracelet for yourself? After that, select a thin yarn. Try using a variety of cords, chains, or yarns to get a wide range of textures and looks in your finished product. You might consider utilizing materials with varying colors, layers, or materials (such as cotton, jute, or nylon) to get the desired appearance. You may add color to your macramé creations by utilizing cords in assorted colors or by including colorful embellishments in your designs. You can add color using yarn, beads, or even dying the cords yourself. Other options include. Investigate the possibility of introducing supplementary components, such as gemstones, shells, feathers, or even little trinkets, into your macramé work. These decorations have the potential to lend your creations more personality and a distinctive style. Macramé is primarily about tying knots, so try various techniques to produce patterns and motifs. Mastering other knots, like the square knot, the half hitch tie, or the spiral knot, will let you widen your skill set and produce more elaborate patterns. Macramé can produce unique patterns and textures by mixing and matching different knotting techniques, including the traditional square knot, horizontal knotting, and the lark's head knot. Combining different techniques can result in some truly breathtaking visual effects.

Consider alternatives to the conventional use of cords and ropes. If you want to give your macramé creations a one-of-a-kind spin, try mixing non-traditional materials such as wire, fabric strips, and other recycled materials into them. You can make your macramé projects the size and shape that best suits your needs by adjusting them.

To create a one-of-a-kind design, you can personalize a pattern by making it bigger or smaller, modifying the shape of your wall hanging, flower hanger, or bracelet, or combining other types of materials. Think about including initials or whole names in your artwork using macramé. Knots can be used to make patterns in the shape of letters, and then letter beads can be added to those patterns to spell forth names or other important words. Get away from conventional symmetry and try experimenting with asymmetrical patterns. Incorporating asymmetry into your macramé designs can help you achieve a contemporary and dynamic look. Look for ideas in the natural world, works of art, or other people's macramé creations. Allow your imagination to go wild as you create your designs and themes. Your macramé creations will certainly be one of a kind if you follow these instructions.

2.2: Inspiration for Creating Unique Designs

Macramé is a craft that can draw inspiration from various disciplines, including historical allusions. Investigating the long and illustrious history of macramé might give you concepts and themes to use in your creations. Reading back to the Victorian era, when complex macramé lacework was frequently employed, is one approach to getting inspiration. This can be done by reading back through history books. Macramé embellishments of such a delicate nature were used on everything from garments to drapes and even jewelry. Researching Victorian macramé designs and methods can give one a sense of the complicated patterns and knots employed during that period. You can then adapt and combine these complex designs and knots into your present macramé creations.

In addition, the revival of macramé in the 1970s is another source of potential motivation. A bohemian and nature-inspired aesthetic was prevalent during that era, as evidenced by the widespread use of jute plant hangers or macramé owl wall hangings. Researching antique macramé design patterns from the 1970s might inspire you to incorporate nostalgic details into your work. Macramé designers can find useful information and ideas on the internet today. Macramé artists and enthusiasts share their works on social media platforms like Instagram and Pinterest. Some of these sites are Instagram and Pinterest. If you want to learn fresh methods, patterns, and ideas for macramé, one of the best ways to do it is to follow macramé-focused accounts on social media, join macramé groups, and interact with other enthusiasts. The natural world is yet another wonderful place to look for ideas. Enjoy nature by taking strolls around parks, botanical gardens, or in your backyard. Take some time to appreciate the beautiful textures and patterns of the flowers, leaves, and other organic forms found in nature. Adding a one-of-a-kind flair to your macramé patterns and tying them to the surroundings can be accomplished by working these natural materials into your patterns. Keep a book of sketches or a computerized mood card where you can gather images, colors, and ideas that excite you and use them later. Create distinctive designs for macramé that reflect your sense of style and individuality by taking inspiration from the world around you, your experiences, and the things that interest you. You will never be at a loss for ideas to use in your macramé creations if you engage in activities such as researching historical references, participating in the macramé community, spending time in nature, and recognizing your creative potential.

2.3: Suggestions to Avoid Common Mistakes

If you use natural fiber items indoors, they are last longer. Macramé wall hangings should be hung so that the center is roughly at eye level. Keep delicate macramé away from fire and odors from cooking. Natural fibers vary in their ability to catch fire, with cotton burning more easily than wool. Keep your macramé away from weather conditions and direct sunlight if you intend to hang it outside. Some macramé cords, like polypropylene cords, are designed expressly for outdoor use and are less susceptible to exposure to sunshine and weather. For hanging instructions, see the section above titled "How to Hang Your Macramé." To remove any dirt or dust, take your macramé item outdoors and give it a gentle shake. Use a soft-bristled brush to gently cover the object's remaining dust and debris. Use a white, fluffy cloth that's been soaked.

Although it's generally not advised to delicately wash macramé, certain pieces, like table runners and placemats, can require more than just a dusting and a quick wipe down. Any macramé products connected to wood, metal, gemstones, or other materials shouldn't be washed. Anything made of macramé with lengthy fringes or motifs that you're concerned might warp or come loose shouldn't go in the washer. Avoid using warm or steaming water, as this could shrink the fabric or create pattern distortion. If hot glue or some fabric adhesive was used to hold the knots in place, either hot or warm water will also affect the adhesion of such materials. Place objects made only of macramé cord within a sack (or a pillowcase with the end tied up with a hair lackey) and wash them briefly in chilly water on the gentle cycle. Use this guidance with extreme care! Place the item on a clean, level surface that won't become harmed by dampness or hang it up to dry in a well-ventilated room away from direct sunlight. Before storing your macramé objects, ensure they are totally dry because any moisture left behind can make them stink and encourage the spread of mold. When your macramé piece comes, hang it up if the fringe is a little knotted or bowed to let gravity help straighten the fringe. Run the tips of your fingers downward through lengthy fringes that haven't been completely combed out to tame the ends and put everything in its proper place. Use a pet massage or comb to brush the fringe to tidy it back up for short fringes. You can steam or iron the fringe if required to remove any kinks. If using an iron, cover the macramé fringe with a tea towel and iron the towel to shield the fiber from direct heat. Avoid any areas with glue since the heat could weaken the bond.

2.4: Online Resources and Macramé Enthusiast Communities

In the digital age, macramé enthusiasts have a wealth of online resources and communities at their fingertips. Whether you are a beginner or an experienced practitioner, these platforms provide inspiration, patterns, instructional videos, and a chance to connect with like-minded individuals. Let's explore some of the popular online resources and communities that can elevate your macramé journey.

Macramé School. Macramé School is a valuable resource for all skill levels. Their website offers a wide range of free instructional videos and designs. From basic knots to intricate patterns, Macramé School provides detailed instructions accompanied by pictures and videos. It's an excellent starting point for beginners looking to learn new techniques and for experienced practitioners seeking fresh ideas and projects.

YouTube. YouTube is a treasure trove of macramé tutorials and project ideas. Numerous creators share their expertise and creativity through instructional clips and inspiring videos. Some popular channels include "Macramé Magic," known for their comprehensive tutorials on various knots and designs, and "Macramé Masterpieces," which showcases stunning macramé projects and offers helpful tips and tricks. The vast selection of content on YouTube ensures that you can continually expand your skills and find endless inspiration.

Instagram. If you're looking for a visually captivating platform to explore macramé creations and connect with fellow enthusiasts, Instagram is the place to be. Countless artists and makers share their macramé masterpieces, innovative designs, and behind-the-scenes glimpses of their creative process. By searching for macramé-related hashtags like #macrame, #macramewallhanging, or #macramecommunity, you can discover amazing artists, lessons, and inspiration. Following and engaging with these accounts will not only keep you updated on the latest trends but also foster a sense of community within the macramé world.

Facebook Groups. Joining macramé-focused Facebook groups allows you to connect with a global community of macramé enthusiasts. These groups provide a platform to share your work, seek advice, and engage in discussions about all things macramé. Consider joining groups like "Macramé Lovers Worldwide," "Knots and Threads: Macramé Community," or "Macramé DIY Projects and Inspiration" to interact with fellow makers, gain insights into new techniques, and stay connected with the evolving macramé scene.

Etsy. When it comes to sourcing materials, purchasing finished macramé creations, or finding unique patterns, Etsy is a go-to online marketplace. Numerous macramé vendors and artists have their stores on Etsy, offering an array of tools, supplies, and finished products. Whether you're looking for premium-quality macramé cords, intricate wall hangings, or downloadable patterns, Etsy provides a vast selection to fuel your macramé endeavors. Supporting independent makers on Etsy not only adds a personal touch to your creations but also contributes to the thriving macramé community.

Macramé Forums. Online forums dedicated to macramé provide a space for in-depth discussions, troubleshooting, and sharing experiences. Platforms like Macramé Forum or Knots and Macramé Community Forum allow you to connect with fellow enthusiasts, seek advice on challenging projects, and share your own insights. Participating in these forums can broaden your knowledge, offer valuable feedback, and foster a sense of camaraderie within the macramé community.

Macramé Blogs. Many macramé enthusiasts and experts maintain blogs where they share tutorials, project ideas, and their personal macramé journey. Exploring these blogs can provide you with a wealth of knowledge and inspiration. Some popular macramé blogs include "The Macramé Maven" and "Knots & Twists," offering step-by-step instructions, pattern downloads, and insightful articles on various macramé topics.

Macramé Workshops and Online Classes. If you prefer hands-on learning and guidance, consider enrolling in macramé workshops or online classes. These learning experiences, often conducted by skilled macramé artists, allow you to dive deeper into specific techniques and projects. Platforms like Skillshare and Udemy offer a wide range of macramé courses that cater to different skill levels and interests.

Macramé Exhibitions and Events. Keep an eye out for local macramé exhibitions, craft fairs, and events in your area. Attending these gatherings provides an opportunity to immerse yourself in the macramé community, meet talented artists, and discover unique macramé creations. Interacting with artists and fellow enthusiasts in person can be a rich and inspiring experience. By exploring these online resources and communities, you can enhance your macramé journey. Engaging with fellow macramé enthusiasts, following tutorials, and finding inspiration will expand your knowledge and creativity.

Remember, macramé is a versatile art form, and the online world is an endless source of learning and collaboration. Embrace the digital age and craft your macramé creations with passion and enthusiasm!

2.5: Answers to Common Questions from Beginners

1. Is learning Macrame simple?

The same thing, a few knots are frequently used in macramé to produce ornamental designs. Once you have learned the fundamental knots, most designs have just these in various combinations. Additionally, most people have tied knots, even if it was simply for their shoelaces. Therefore, there is already something comfortable about the procedure. I strive to make each step in my instructions and kits as easy to follow as possible by breaking it down into smaller activities.

2. How much thread or cable will I need to do Macrame?

Almost anything may be used to make macramé! Any string or rope can be used for Macrame, as well as wire and ribbon if you choose. However, some macrame ropes, cords, and threads are frequently employed. Typically, macrame cords fit into either of these groups. A "single twist" is a collection of fine threads braided together to resemble a chunkier, softer variant of domestic string. It produces a nice finish and is excellent for making tassels or fringe. Rope gives your Macrame additional texture because it has three twisted threads, which is why it is also known as a 3-ply rope. Since it is also simpler to manage when you start yet still produces a decent fringe, I frequently use 3-ply rope in my kits. The cord is often braided for bigger macrame creations, usually around a core. Cotton is the most common material used to make macrame cord, string, and rope because it tightly clings the knots. NOTE: The phrases string, rope, and cord can all be used in a loose sense. I often refer to the cord as a blanket phrase. Single twist, ply, and braided are good indicators of the cable you need.

3. How much string or cable do I need for macramé?

This depends on the materials you are using and the cord's thickness. However, you frequently utilize more than you realize you need. The best course of action for a novice macrame maker is to follow tutorials and designs or purchase an instructional kit that includes instructions on how much cord to use for each item. You'll start to get an understanding of the lengths of cable required for various applications.

However, if you pressed me for a reply, I would suggest working under the assumption that each string should be at least 2 meters long for little jewelry pieces and 4 meters long for big wall hangings. Although this won't work for each style, it's a decent place to start.

4. Do I require a lot of equipment and tools when starting?

Macrame is fantastic because it doesn't require a lot of tools or specialized equipment. Your own hands are the primary equipment! However, there are a few items that will make macrame-making simpler. Making knots typically requires having something that will keep your work in place. You only need some washi or masking tape to tape the cords to your desk to achieve this. A foam or string board might be very handy for tiny-scale items. You can use regular sewing pins or more durable macrame t-pins to secure the rope to the board.

Some specially designed boards from foam also feature slots around the perimeter to secure cords. You will need standard household materials to measure your cord, such as stitching measuring tape or flexible metal DIY tape. To cut the strings and trim your fringes, use sharp scissors. And all you need is a cheap plastic comb to remove the fringe.

5. What can I construct with Macrame?

I used to believe that Macrame was just used to create wall-hanging owls and plant hangers. But Macrame is highly adaptable and might be used to make anything from jewelry to room dividers to garments and cushion covers.

Chapter 3: Beginner Projects

3.1: Keyring

Keychains made of macramé are an extremely easy craft for beginners. They need a few materials and the fundamental knowledge and methods for knotting the macrame cords.

These keychains may be made in copious quantities, so keep them around to serve as gifts for parties or little presents for Mother's Day or Friendship Day. Purchase some macrame rope in the shade you like or create a two-color keychain.

Supplies and Equipment You'll Need

But first, you must collect your materials so that you may begin. Here are the things you'll need:

- key chain
- (32'' long) 3x 4mm triple twist cotton cords
- Sellotape Scissors
- Beads

- embroidery floss

- hairbrush

Instructions

With the ring secured, you may continue working on the DIY task without being concerned about how that ring keeps falling out of place.

1. Bring the ends of one of the cords together as you bend it in half. This kind of loop will be at the other end.

2. Pull the loop through the lock ring and then beneath it.

3. Pull both cords around the ring to form a lark's head knot if you are comfortable with various macrame knots.

4. But don't worry if you don't know what the macrame words for various knots mean!

5. Pull the loop down one more to settle it precisely over the metal after you've passed it through the ring and beneath it. The two end cords should then be gathered and pulled through the loop by putting a finger through it.

6. To tighten the connection around the ring, pull the wires through and then pull on them. Ta-da! Your first lark's head knot has been created.

7. You need to repeat this procedure with one of the two cables, and you're ready to begin developing your design.

8. Divide the six cables into three pieces next. The middle two cables should be taped to the work surface.

9. You'll combine many "square knots" to create this specific pattern. To create a loop that resembles a "4", first take the two wires on the left, then position them over the center wires.

10. Next, take the cables on the right, then attach them to the left-hand cords.

11. Do you see where the center and left cables intersect at that point? Pull the right cables through the opening you created with the left wires and beneath the crossover you built.

12. Now make the first half of the square knot by pulling the ends of both cords in opposing directions and moving towards the circle as you do so.

13. You will now tie the identical knot, but you will pull the cords to the right to create the loop around the center cords this time.

14. After that, cross the left cables over the right ones and draw the ends of the cords through the circle you have created.

15. To make the knot more secure, tug on the cord's ends. Under the first knot you tied, secure this second one. Together, these two knots form a square knot.

16. We will add beads to liven up your keychain before you continue. The ends of both center cables must be taped to do this. They will be simpler to pierce through the bead as a result.

17. After pulling it through, place the bead beneath your initial square knot at the top.

18. Tie other square knots to keep the bead in place after that. Just start using the cables on the left because you know the routine!

19. Just keep descending as you normally would. Place a bead and finish off with a square knot after every square knot. Once you've gotten the hang of it, it's simple.

20. You ought to have a series of five knots that are square with four beads inserted between them to give readers an idea. When you're finished and satisfied with the length, it's time to wrap it up.

21. Cut a piece of embroidery floss using a pair of scissors. Use an opposite hue if you'd like, or feel free to utilize the same color thread as the cotton cord.

22. Pull the opposite end of the connecting thread when the thread's up-facing end faces the cables to form a U-shape.

23. You can gather all the cords by wrapping the other tip of a thread around the tip of the final rectangular knot and holding that U-shaped knot in place.

24. Once you are satisfied with the thickness, keep wrapping the thread around.

25. Pull the end of the cable you just wrapped through the U-loop by grabbing it.

26. Hold both ends and pull them in opposing directions to fix the wrapping in place.

27. Snip off both ends last.

28. You're almost finished! Cut the cords' ends equally, then comb them out with a comb.

3.2: Fruit Hammock

Supplies You'll Need

- 12 pieces of 5 mm crochet string that is 90 inches long.

- 2 wooden dowels measuring 12 inches each and 1/4 inch thick (may need to be chopped down to fit underneath your cabinet)

- 4 Command hooks or 4 screw-on hooks.

- Sharp scissors and craft glue

- Sandpaper and a hacksaw (if you're chopping down dowels)

Instructions

1. First, attach cords to a single dowel.

2. Use a lark's head knot to fasten one of the ropes to one on the dowels.

3. Tie additional hitch knots on the opposite side and left to create an extended lark's head knot.

4. With the remaining cables, repeat that action. This will form a sturdy knot that will serve as our foundation.

5. Tie alternate square knots in step two.

6. Using tape, fasten the dowel to the work area.

7. When you have six square knots for the first row, tie the first one to the left and work your way across.

8. Give the row of square knots and the dowel approximately a finger's breadth of separation.

9. As you descend, skip the first and second strings and tie five square knots that run across. Between every square knot in the preceding row, these will be placed.

10. Alternating square knots are what are used in this. Moreover, you will omit the last two chords.

11. Up until there are 15 rows total, repeat rows 1 and 2. This will serve as the hammock's body.

12. Fasten the rope ends to the second dowel.

13. Lay the second dowel over the cords' straightened-out ends between each row of square knots.

14. Use the double half hitch knots to fasten each rope to the second dowel, traveling from left to right. The distance between the final row of knots that are square, and the dowel should be around a finger's breadth.

15. Tie off the extra cored and cut it.

16. To make the double-quarter hitch knots more secure, flip the paracord hammock toward the back and tie them again.

17. Apply a line of adhesive all over the double ½ hitch knots' backs. The glue should now be spread out so that it covers the knots' backs using your index finger or a paintbrush. Dry it out. Grab a set of scissors and trim the string's long end near the knots after the glue has completely dried.

18. Ensure that the cables are sufficiently apart to span the same quantity of dowels while holding the two dowels together. If they aren't even, spread your knots on the double-quarter hitch.

19. You must now choose between using screw-in hooks and Command-strip hooks. How permanent you'd like your macrame basket for fruits to be will determine how to proceed.

20. Additionally, if you're like me and opted to test fit the hammock later (oops!), you'll have to test fit it now to check whether the dowel has to be trimmed down.

21. Okay, now choose a location for your hammock's left side. Attach both command hooks and screw into the hooks onto that side. Continue on the right side.

3.3: Fringed Macrame Coasters

This project produces 4 coasters.

Supplies

- Grey and black 3mm single ply macrame cords, each around 9 meters long.

- textile shears

- a 14" thick x 8" long piece of wood

- Ruler

Instructions

- One coaster may be made using these directions.

- Cut the string into eight 28"-long sections. You need four of each hue.

- A LARK'S HEAD KNOT should be used to secure each component to the wooden dowel.

- Fold your cord half, then loop it over the dowel to form a Lark's Head Knot. Bring the two sides through the loop after carrying it around the back. Tighten the cable. After doing this for each of them, Center all 8 cord pieces on the dowel.

- The first row of knots should be tied after a spacing of 1/2" from the dowel.

- Every four cords in the first row, knot a SQUARE KNOT.

- Bring cord 1 beneath cord 4 and over the extra cords (2 and 3). Cord 4 passes via cords 1 and 2 before passing below the fillers. Pull firmly.

- Place cord 4 under cord 1 and over the filler cords (2 and 3). Cord 1 ascends via cords 3 and 4 and beneath fillers. Pull firmly.

- Use neither the first nor the final two cords in the subsequent row of knots. Move them to the side. For every four cords, tie a square knot.

- One of your square knots will be grey, and the next square knotted in the following row will blend grey and black.

- Four black cords will tie the third tie in the second row.

- When your Macrame is 4" long on the wood dowel, repeat steps 3 and 4.

- As you can see, I tied four rows with knots using the same color yarn for each tie (repeating Step 3), as you see for my coasters. Grey or black square knots alternately appear amid the rows of knots between each other (repeating Step 4).

- To prevent unraveling, securely tie the last row of square knots.

- Cut through the center of each lark's head knot (also known as the yarn, which is parallel to the dowel and used as the loop for constructing the knot) to remove the Macrame from the dowel.

- On the two ends of the coaster, unravel the whole fringe.

- Trim the fringe ends to an equal length of approximately 1" on each end.

Chapter 4: Macramé for Home Decor & Outdoor Spaces

Macrame is a simple addition that can be made to any room to make it feel more open and spacious. Because of its subtle knots and muted tones, it will lend an air of refined elegance to any setting. Macrame may be incorporated into your home decor in many ways, ranging from subtle touches, such as plant hangers, to bold statements, such as hanging chairs.

4.1: Ideas for Using Macramé to Decorate Your Living Space

We have gathered a variety of macrame concepts for you to examine, including both prefabricated and do-it-yourself options, which will motivate you for your subsequent macrame project or acquisition for your living area.

1. A Mini Macrame

In addition to its adorable appearance, the tiny macrame wall hanging is versatile, and you can have fun experimenting with it. If you would like a wall to abide out and make most strongly of your small Macrame, I suggest placing it close to a larger portion. This will allow you to make the most of its potential. It may be a reduced form of a larger item with the same hue but a unique assortment of cotton strings, or it may feature the same scenario but a unique shade of yarn. If you have a passion for Macrame and enjoy experimenting with new creative ideas, another option is to hang it on the wall next to various things of varying sizes and shapes.

For instance, you might display it in two picture frames of different sizes or shapes, and if you're feeling bold and enjoy bright colors, use bright ones to give it a current pop effect; this could be perfect for a teen room or to provide character to a wall that is otherwise very bland. If you are unsure, I suggest you experiment by trying several choices using tape before finalizing the look. If you don't feel fulfilled with the result, you will not destroy your good wall, particularly for macrame projects intended for children's rooms. A miniature wall hanging is ideal for a nursery or a child's room.

2. A Cushion

Pillows are a wonderful method to give an instant boost and revitalize a worn-out look on a budget, in addition to contributing to the overall aesthetic of a room. On a couch, the optimal number of pillows is five, and while you have a variety of options available to you in terms of size, texture, and color, you should keep in mind the overall design aesthetic of the space. The fact that a macrame cushion may have a variety of textures and colors simultaneously is one of the many reasons why it is such an eye-catching addition to any space. If you want to give a space an immediate rich impression, make sure that you use an extremely soft string rather than cable (maybe reed string/cotton), choose neutral colors, and if you are crafting your own, don't mix more than three colors. If you maintain an old pillow, you should consider repurposing it using Macrame. If you are daring and want to add something more, why not paint the cords with the natural dyes you have made yourself?

3. A wreath made of Macrame.

Are you able to enjoy it to its fullest? This excellent macrame item might be used for a long time and restyled for various events. If you don't already have one, you should start making one immediately! Choose colors that go with the rest of your decorating, and if they use neutrals, you'll be able to quickly "dress it up" for extraordinary events such as Easter, Christmas, and or maybe a baby shower or use it as a unique touch to your special day decoration!

It looks amazing perched above a fireplace, but during the holiday season, you can consider moving it to the front entrance or placing it behind the Christmas tree and highlighting it with fairy lights or greenery to draw attention to it.

4.2: Wall Hangings

The following are the directions for producing a basic macramé wall hanging in the step-by-step format:

Supplies

- A cord for macramé

- Dowel made of wood, or a ring made of metal for hanging.

- Scissors

- Measuring tape.

Instructions

1. To achieve the look you want; cut numerous pieces of macramé rope to the length you want. The dimensions and weight of your hang hanging will determine the number of cables you will need. After folding each rope in half, you must thread it through the oak dowel or the metal ring. This results in a knot known as a lark's head. Carry on until your cords are fastened to your chosen rod or ring. Create pairs out of the cords that are separated. Using the cord from your initial pair as a starting point and the cord with the second pair as the target, tie a diagonal half-hitch loop around the cord with the first pair.

2. Continue following these steps with each set of cords until you approach the proper side of the object. To make a perfectly straight base row, tighten the knots equally. The length of this row will define how wide your wall hanging will be. After that, you may start making different knots out of macramé to add some texture and design.

3. Square tying and circular knots are the most prevalent types. To create the desired pattern, you must try various knotting techniques, combinations, and configurations.

4. You can mix and match the knots, build rows of one particular knot, or alternate between the two. Remember to hang a little extra cord extension at the bottom of your wall to add fringes.

5. You can cut them afterward into fringe patterns such as V-shapes or diagonal cuts or trim them to the length you want. In addition, you can include additional components such as beads, feathers, and other shells by stringing them onto separate ropes and attaching them with knots.

6. After you are satisfied with the design you have created with macramé, trim any excess string to produce a sleek and clean edge.

You may also use a comb with wide or thumbs to comb along the cords to straighten up and fluff them, giving your wall hanging the appearance of completion.

7. Make a loop at the very top of each wooden splinter or metal ring by using an additional piece of cord that you have on hand. This loop will act as the hanger for the object. Find a place on your wall that is ideal for hanging your macramé wall hanging, then insert a hook or nail into the wall.

8. Remember that the following directions provide a general framework for your work. Still, you can try different approaches, exercise your imagination, and adapt the layout to better fit your needs. Macramé is a diverse art form, so have fun with the process of creating your one-of-a-kind wall hanging and enjoy the process!

4.3: Plant Hangers

They have come to the correct place if they've always wanted to learn how to construct their macrame plant container!

This easy macramé pot hanger pattern can be constructed with just a few basic knotting techniques, making it a brilliant choice for beginners starting with macramé. If they follow the steps in this guide, they will be able to create a custom piece of decor for their home that is unique!

Supplies

- Macrame plant hanger
- Cotton cord designed with Macrame.
- A small plant pot is required.
- Terracotta pot 4.5 inches in height and 5 inches around.

Instructions

1. To tie a loop rather than a ring, one of the cords will be somewhat longer than the others. It is recommended that they cut one length of cord that is 19 feet long and five pieces of cord that are 13 feet long.

2. After the cables have been cut, it is frequently suggested to use some masking tape to secure the cut ends to prevent the cords from unraveling. To begin the macrame plant hanger, there are a few diverse ways. Here are two easy procedures to follow.

3. To begin with a ring, The ring should be suspended from a hook or secured to the surface of a table. Each of the ropes should be run through the ring until they are all finished. The two ends of the cords should be brought together so that they are even on both sides, and then the ring should be placed so that the center of the rope's rests on it.

4. Three square knots should be made with two outermost cords, and those square knots should be tied around the remaining ten cords. Each five shorter ropes should be folded in half to locate the middle.

5. A pencil or a piece of tape can be used to indicate where the center point is. The ropes should be unfolded and placed horizontally on a table. The longer rope should be folded in half lengthwise to locate the middle. A Lark's Head Knot should be made using the five shorter cords gathered. Ten Vertical Lark's Head Knots should be created with the available cord.

6. To tie a square knot, the working cord on the left should be brought under the working cord on the right, then brought back over the two filler cords. The right working cord should be brought over the filler cords and under the left working cord, then brought back over the left working cord. It should be tightened. The right working cord should be brought under the left working cord after passing it over the filler cords and to the left.

7. The working cord on the left should be placed over the two filler cords and then brought back over the working cord on the right. The knot should be pulled closer together. The first square knot has been successfully tied. The height should be reduced by 6 inches.

8. Perform a series of twenty half-square knots with the first group of cords being worked with. This pattern should be repeated with each group of cords until a complete round of spiral knots has been tied. Continue tying square knots followed by spiral knots in alternating fashion.

9. After finishing the round of spiral knots, move down another 6 inches and repeat the process. Make a square knot with the first group of cords. Continue with the next bunch of cords, creating a spiral knot. Alternate between square and spiral knots with each bunch of cords until another round has been completed.

10. Continue tying alternate knots, then measure the length of the string. Continue alternating between square and spiral knots, going down 6 inches after each round until reaching the desired length. Make sure to alter the number of knots in each round to achieve the desired design and spacing. After several rounds, they can hold up their plant pot to see if the length is sufficient. Modifications should be made, as necessary.

11. Once the required length for the plant hanger has been achieved, all the cords should be gathered together. A gathering knot should be tied at the bottom to bind all the cords together. The excess cord below the gathering knot should be trimmed to achieve a neat finish. The plant pot should be placed into the macramé hanger and adjusted to the correct height.

12. It should be ensured that the hanger supports the pot firmly and evenly. A hook or nail should be attached to the selected spot on the wall or ceiling.

The loop or ring located at the very top of the macramé plant hanger should be used. It should be checked that the hanger is stable and level before using it. After adding the plant of choice to the pot, the lovely macramé plant hanger can be admired.

4.4: Creating Macramé Pieces Suitable for Gardens, Patios, And Balconies

The craft of macramé provides infinite opportunities to create spectacular and one-of-a-kind objects that can improve the visual appeal of outdoor spaces such as gardens, balconies, and balconies. Macramé is an elaborate knotting that may decorate outdoor areas with a touch of natural beauty because of the wonderful textures it creates. Imagine a variety of colorful plants being hung from elaborately crafted macramé planting hangers so that they move gracefully in the wind. These one-of-a-kind works of handicrafts give an elegant and beautiful method for displaying your favorite potted plants, producing an aesthetically pleasant point of interest in your yard or other outdoor space. Macramé may also be employed to build hanging chairs and hammocks, which provide a quaint and pleasant place to unwind and take in the beauty of the outdoors. These macramé masterpieces offer both practicality and aesthetics, letting you chill in style while benefiting from their construction's long-lasting and strong strands. Macramé wall hangings are an excellent solution for people with restricted areas outside their homes. These elaborate textiles can be hung on walls, fencing, or even the exteriors of balconies, so transforming an otherwise ordinary surface into a breathtaking exhibition of artistic prowess. Macramé wall hangings offer various patterns and styles, giving your outdoor space a touch of boho allure or a modern air of refinement.

The fact that macramé may be used for various projects is one of the craft's many strengths. It is possible to make it out of various materials, like cotton, jute, or possibly recycled ropes, which allows you to customize the appearance and texture of the macramé pieces you use outside. Your macramé creations can take on a genuinely one-of-a-kind look by including personal touches like beads, feathers, and other unique embellishments, which you can achieve by experimenting with various knotting techniques. Incorporating macramé into your outdoor design may lend a feeling of artistic expression and enhance your space's natural beauty. This is true regardless of the size of your outdoor area, be it a large garden, a cozy patio, or a cramped balcony. Macramé is a great craft that enables you to embellish your garden areas with elegance, charm, and a touch of your creative touch.

With its classic allure and limitless design opportunities, macramé is a craft that will stand the test of time.

4.5: Hammocks, And Swing Chairs

Following are the instructions Hammock chair, wall hanging and swing chair.

Supplies

- Macrame cord

- Dowel is made of wood.

- Metal ring for hanging the scissors.

Instructions

1. Macramé cord should be cut into eight pieces, each roughly 12-14 feet long. After folding each rope in half, use a lark's wing knot to secure it and loop it through the metal ring or wooden dowel.

2. Gather all of the cords into one place, then tie a large knot in the topmost part of the bundle, ensuring to leave a few extra inches of cord will be left for hanging.

3. Separate the cords into their four respective pairs.

4. After tying the top knot, working with each combination, tie square-knotted or spiraling knots approximately two to three feet down towards the top knot.

5. Continue the pattern of the knots along the entire length of the cords, leaving enough room in the middle for an easy sitting place.

6. A collecting knot, or another ornamental knot should be used to finish off the bottom.

7. Ensure the macramé suspension chair is safely anchored by suspending it from a strong beam or nail in your outside space and hanging it there.

4.6: Outdoor Wall Hanging

Cord for macramé projects that can be used outside (such as nylon, polyester, or other materials resistant to the elements), a hanging device made of a wooden peg or driftwood.

Supplies

- Macrame cord, each measuring roughly 4-6 feet in

Instructions

1. Make a lark's head knot with each cord, then attach them to the driftwood or wooden dowel. Use a variety of macramé knots, such as circular knots, spiral knots, or diagonal knots, to create the pattern and design that best suits your needs. If you choose, you can accessorize the necklace with feathers, beads, and shells.

2. you may create a neat edge by trimming any excess cord after creating your design. Hooks or nails can be used to put the macramé fence hanging on an outside wall or fence, and you should make sure the hanging is fastened firmly.

3. consider the various external factors and select materials appropriate for usage outside. In addition, you should routinely inspect your macramé components for any cryptograms of wear and tear and make any necessary changes or repairs to guarantee their durability and ensure that they are safe to use in your garden, on your patio, or on your balcony.

4. Macramé is an enjoyable craft that can be used to create lovely pieces that may be used to improve your outdoor space.

Chapter 5: Macramé Jewelry Making

5.1: Techniques for creating macramé earrings

Making these lovely Macrame earrings is a quick and straightforward process that requires extraordinarily little time. The technique is simple, allowing you to design them in a way that reflects your unique personality and incorporates them into your jewelry.

Once you've gathered the necessary components, all left to do is go through the processes outlined in this paragraph.

Supplies

- Cotton Rope with a Single Strand Diameter of 4mm

- 2x jump rings.

- two sets of earring hooks

- four beads of your choosing

- a piece of tape (or clips)

- Scissors

- Hair comb

Instructions

1. First, take the long thread and fold it into half lengthwise. This is the first stage in the process. This is the thread or spine that runs through the center of the earring. Hold on to the jump ring, as we will require it for the step after this one.

2. Thread the jump ring into the folded spine to make a cotton circle at the project's highest point.

3. Bring the loop from the top down to overlap the jump ring where it was previously attached. It needs to be positioned on top of both unfastened strings.

4. Thread the threads that are loose through the loop. It should result in a knot at the head. Now, to make it more secure, tighten the knot. After you have ensured that the knot remains taut, you are free to proceed to the following step.

5. Then use the adhesive or a clip to secure the top of your earrings to remain stable while you complete the remaining stages. To tie one knot, you will want two shorter threads, one for each side of the spine.

6. Insert one of the curled short strings into the space between the spine and the back panel. Take the next one, bend it in half so that it has a loop, and then place that loop into the ring at the top of the horizontal strand.

7. Pull the additional string through (but don't let it travel all the way through) and put it vertically atop the first strand in the other direction.

8. Thread the untied ends of your bottom threads through the highest loop completely.

9. After drawing both sides securely, Step 9 should result in a strong knot being formed.

10. Change the beginning side to the following step, step 10 of the process. For instance, if you begin the first one right to left (which will result in a loop being created on the right), you should begin the second one going left to right (which would result in the loop being created on the left).

11. Proceed with the steps again, as described above. Place the first strand that has been folded below the spine. Insert another string that has been doubled into the loop.

12. To make the top strand snugger, thread the free ends of the bottom strands around the loop formed by the top strand. Repeat these steps as often as necessary until you have enough strands to form the feather shape.

13. Proceed by decreasing the size of each step progressively. After you tie each knot, you must ensure the strands are pulled up and tightened.

14. It is important not to leave spaces between the knots since this will prevent the feather from becoming thick enough. Before trimming it, comb through the hair to separate the strands.

15. After brushing the strands to eliminate excessive knots or folds, go to the next step and rough trim the ends. Because it is just an outline now, you shouldn't be too concerned if it isn't perfect yet.

16. Not only does this assist in shaping the form, but it also makes it much simpler to brush the hair out of the way. When you brush it out, it will be much simpler to do so if the strands are shorter.

17. After giving each strand a rough trim, begin brushing the threads to separate every thread and loosen the rope to create the silky feel of a feather. This should be done after you have given the strands a rough trim. Brushing outwards, beginning at the spine, and working your way toward the ends, is required as you normally brush your hair.

18. When brushing, make a strong effort to push into the cording to disentangle the twist. Begin from the very top and work your way to the bottom.

19. While detangling the lower sections, hold the base of the spine in your hand to protect it from the power of the brushing. The spine is fragile, and you do not want the knot to go undone as you work.

20. You should have a fundamental framework after carrying out the procedure on both sides. At this point, you should be able to view each thread, as seen in the photo below.

21. Before finishing the trim, you can add beads of your choosing. This is an extra step that is completely voluntary.

22. You are under no need to include it, but I believe doing so would be a fantastic opportunity to inject more of your unique personality into your writing. It adds that additional facet to make it unique.

23. The next step is to thread the beads through. Pick the colors that appeal to you the most. It is sufficient with two beads.

24. After threading the beads through the hole, cut another short string to fasten them.

25. Tie a thumb loop at the bracelet's base to keep the beads from falling out. Pull the knot's ends closer together to ensure it is secure.

26. Comb the last thread, and then give the hair its final cut. Be overly cautious when cutting since this is the most difficult aspect of the process. How you slice the feather is extremely crucial since this will affect its overall form.

27. You may make the threads more rigid by using water or a stiffener. This not only makes it much simpler to cut but also strengthens the thread and helps it last longer.

28. After you have completed the last bit of trimming, wait for it to dry for a while.

29. You now have a unique pair of earrings set to be included in your subsequent outfit of the day (OOTD)!

5.2: Necklace

The secret to this necklace is that you only need one cord to make the braid, rather than three separate ones, and you can achieve a fancy-looking plait by double-tying the string! You can also turn it into jewelry if a necklace isn't your style.

The following materials are required:

- Cord.

- 2 meters (about 2.2 yards) of 4mm 3ply linen macramé cord.

- Tape measure

- Washi, masking, or painter's tape

- scissors,

- two jump rings,

- two 7mm fold-over under ends, and a clasp.

- Pliers

Instructions

1. Cut a two m piece of string, then fold it over twice. Use tape to secure the rope that has been doubled to the tabletop. To make our braid, leave the leftover cord at your bottom and around 25 cm at the highest point (above the tape).

2. Using the lengthy end, create a loop by looping it under itself immediately below the tape and then back up on the right.

3. Finish with the lengthy portion on the right after bringing the end back to the right as you go through the loop.

4. Now that you have three cords to work with, you can plait your hair precisely like that! Bring the rope on the left to the center to begin.

5. Insert the correct cable into the center. Keep the cables that have been doubled up flat adjacent to one another.

6. Pull the long tail through the loop formed by the remaining two cords to untangle the ends, which will be slightly twisted. I've discovered that placing a finger on the braiding prevents it from buckling.

7. If you are familiar with braiding hair, you might discover it simpler to take it up at this stage and start a braid.

8. Continue braiding until you hit bottom, bringing the left chord into the center before moving on to the right.

9. Bringing the extended end into the center, simply a loop on the bottom is the last step to complete the braid. It is usually preferable to do the final move with some extra space than to attempt to make it very tight.

10. Working your way back up, softly pull the parts apart to neaten the braiding.

11. Gently bend the braiding, paying attention to the cords to ensure they are not twisted. The length of the braided segment will be around 13 cm. To complete the remainder of the necklace, you should have a 20 to 25-cm cord on each side. Each side of mine is 15 cm shorter, thanks to me. The necklace length was 45cm (18″) when the ends plus clasp were attached.

12. Attach the folded-over ends to the string and add the clasp by folding one end down, finally the other, and then firmly clamping with pliers to fasten. Both ends should be done.

13. Cut out any extra cable at either end.

14. Add the clasp to one end with one jump ring and the other with the second one so it can latch onto it.

15. Just fasten the fold-over ends at the very end of each braiding to transform it into a necklace!

5.3: Bracelets

You'll need a connector or charms or both.

You'll also need.

- 4 yards or 0.5mm

- Chinese tying cord.

- a lighter (optional).

- a set of flat noses pliers.

- a pair of scissors.

- an embroidery needles.

Instructions

1. Cut the knotting string into four lengths: two 30-inches, two 20-inches, and one 10-inch. Folding the 20-inch strip in half and pulling the loop around the ring before folding it onto it to complete the closure. On the other end of the ring, repeat the action. These threads will be fixed in place and secured.

2. Under both of the middle strands, center the 30-inch cable. Fold the opposite cord under the left cord and over the center strands. Pull both left cords through the opening on the opposite side and beneath the right and center strands.

3. Slide the tie up to the highest point by pulling firmly.

4. Folding a left cord across the center strands underneath the right cord completes the second part of the square knot. Pull the opposite end of the cord through the opening on the left side, beneath the center and left strands.

5. Repeat the steps by pulling firmly: left, right, left, right. Up until the required length is obtained, keep knotting. Remember that the link will occupy around half an inch.

6. Put one of these cords on a needle and stitch up the middle of three to four knots around the back to complete the knots. The needle may be pushed into tight knots with the aid of pliers.

7. On the other cord, carry out the same procedure.

8. Trim any extra cord after stitching up both knotting cords. Keep the leftovers and use a lighter to melt the tips to seal them for added grip. Carry out the same procedure on the other side of the bracelet.

9. Make the bracelet appear circular, then overlap the center strands to create a sliding closing. To temporarily knot the cords up at either end, use scraps.

10. Center the 10-inch cord below the strands. Start making square knots in the same manner as the bracelet.

11. Stop and stitch the tying cords into the closure's reverse when you reach approximately half an inch. Take off the bridging ties.

12. The bracelet's adjustable ties are now the two pairs of middle strands. Tie knots in both ends and adjust to suit the wrist. Remove any surplus.

13. You've completed your adjustable knotted bracelets.

5.4: Beads and charms into your jewelry design

Make this bracelet with the following:

- To match the beads, use white yarn.

- Scissors.

- All-purpose adhesive

- Beads, a little under double the number for a standard bracelet

Instructions

1. Cut the yarn twice around your wrist. Cut another equal-length piece. Knot the two strands.

2. This bracelet section will be macrame-knotted. I like two strands since one makes a skinny bracelet.

3. Both strands need a foundation bead.

4. Take scissors and yarn again. Cut after twenty wraps.

5. You have a foundation and a very lengthy strand. Half-fold the strand. Place the center behind the base. Hold the center with your thumb. Place the right thread over the foundation and beneath the left. Put the left strands beneath the base and up into the right-side loop. Pull both threads together gently. Before tightening, situate the knot under the bead.

6. Your knot has a vertical line to the left and a yarn across the base to the right. Put the end over the base from this line's left side. Like the previous knot, put the strand below the base and up through the loop on the opposite side.

7. Bead both strands to begin.

8. The vertical line appears on the right, so start by placing the right strands over the base. As with ordinary knots, pass the left strand underneath the base and through the loop. Keep your beads in place as indicated in the photographs.

9. Step 5 describes the following knot, which is straightforward.

10. Repeat step 6.

11. yellow-orange-red-pink-purple-dark-light blue green

12. Repeat until your wrist measures a few centimeters sans beads.

13. Knot the lengthy outside strands tight to the bracelet. Put the threads through the second-last bead knot. (Check out the photos)

14. Turn the bracelet over and tie the two strands. Pull it firmly and glue it.

15. Mark the height of the string without a bead on your wrist.

16. Take any of the yarn pieces you cut from the previous step. Like the previous knot, fold it in half to reach the center. The next section is like the previous knot but with four strands. Place the center behind the line and the starting point of the macrame (aligned). Make the knot as you did use the first knot.

17. Make eleven additional knots for a lovely twelve-knot item. Just follow the usual knot directions from the instructor.

18. Cut the strands you tied and attach them to the twelve knots. Don't attach this portion to the base; otherwise, the bracelet won't be adjustable. Cut the base end to match the initial length. Add a knot and bead.

19. The first two photographs illustrate how far the bracelet can be lengthened, while the rest are merely additional pictures.

5.5: Macramé Anklet with Beads Beads

Make this anklet with the following:

- 2mm cotton cord

- Beads of your choice

- Scissors

- Tape measure

Instructions

- Cut two pieces of cotton cord, each measuring approximately 90 cm in length.

- Fold both cords in half and align the ends.

- Tie a knot at the folded end of the cords, leaving a loop large enough to fit around your ankle.

- Secure the loop by attaching it to a surface with tape or using a clipboard.

- Separate the cords into four groups, with two cords in each group.

- Starting from the left, take the outer left cord and cross it over the two middle cords, forming a "4" shape.

- Take the outer right cord and cross it over the left cord, passing it through the loop created by the left cord.

- Pull both cords to tighten the knot.

- Repeat steps 6-8 with the remaining cords, working from left to right, until you reach the desired length for your anklet. Make sure to leave enough space at the end to tie a secure knot.

- String a bead onto one cord from each pair, sliding it up to the last knot.

- Tie a knot below the bead to secure it in place. Repeat this step with the remaining cords and beads.

- To finish the anklet, tie all the cords together in a tight knot, leaving a small loop for the closure.

- Trim any excess cord, leaving a short fringe if desired.

- Your macramé anklet with beads is now ready to wear!

5.6: Macramé Ring with Beaded Accent

Make this ring with the following:

- 2mm cotton cord

- Bead of your choice

- Scissors

- Tape measure

Instructions

- Cut a piece of cotton cord measuring approximately 90 cm in length. Fold the cord in half and align the ends.

- Tie a knot at the folded end of the cord, leaving a small loop at the top for the ring. Secure the loop by attaching it to a surface with tape or using a clipboard. Separate the cords into four groups, with two cords in each group. Starting from the left, take the outer left cord and cross it over the two middle cords, forming a "4" shape.

- Take the outer right cord and cross it over the left cord, passing it through the loop created by the left cord. Pull both cords to tighten the knot.

- Repeat these steps with the remaining cords, working from left to right, until you have created a small macramé section.

- Slide a bead onto the four cords, positioning it above the macramé section.

- Tie a knot below the bead to secure it in place.

- Continue knotting the cords in the same pattern as before, creating additional macramé sections if desired.

- When you reach the desired size for your ring, tie all the cords together in a tight knot.

- Trim any excess cord, leaving a short fringe if desired.

- Gently shape the ring to fit your finger, adjusting the size as needed.

- Your macramé ring with a beaded accent is now complete!

Chapter 6: Macramé for Special Occasions

Why not give making your macramé items a shot if you want to add that special touch of individuality to your big day? You may make everything from background for your ceremony to placemats or a table runner for reception, bouquet wraps, table plan wall hanging, chair decorations, or plant hangers as a green wall well before the big day.

6.1: How to Use Macramé to Add a Personal Touch to Weddings, Parties, And Events

It is simple to accomplish with guidance from YouTube videos or by enrolling in a class. If you aren't feeling very inventive, your best bet is to hire or get the items you need. There are people in this world that, if you are seeking something that is completely one of a kind, you can contract to make whatever you want to have made.

Although macramé may be used in many different areas of your wedding, having a macramé wedding backdrop or arch is one of the most beautiful and eye-catching ways to make a great impression on your big day. You have some options available to you for how to style it. If the ceremony is held inside, you can affix it to the wall, and if it is held outside, you can suspend it from an oak or an arch. A straightforward arch may be transformed into an eye-catching focal point simply by adding a macramé hanging to its surface; voila, your arch is finished, and what a remarkable impression it will create! Depending on the style you are going for, the macramé hanging may drape across the entire arch or cover a portion of it. Although you could consider adding some intertwined foliage or blooms to your bouquet to accent it, a gorgeous macramé piece does not need anything added. To finish the photo, put a couple of candles or lanterns behind the subject, which will help highlight the background even more. In the same vein as the rest of your wedding decor, strive to personalize your engagement arch with as much detail as possible. Not only does this help your wedding reflect who you are as a couple, but it also helps round out the vision you have been working towards for your big day.

As you walk down the aisle, imagine this amazing feature is waiting for you; what an unbelievable manner it would be for you to say your wedding vows! Angela Daley, a local expert in macramé and owner of Hygge Crafter, created this stunning piece as a one-of-a-kind commission for the couple. It was custom-made to suit and match our straightforward wooden arbor, and it was the ideal background for a backyard wedding. Therefore, if you are considering having a wedding in the bohemian style, you might think about incorporating some macrame decoration into your big day. Macramé is a stunning and inexpensive method to make the wedding day stand out from others, and it can do it in many ways, from a single standout piece to a whole overhaul of an area.

6.2: Table Runners

Following are the instructions for Table Runners and Backdrops made with Macrame.

Supplies

- Wooden dowel measuring 12 inches in diameter.

- 22 strands of cotton ropes measuring 3 millimeters each

- over-the-door hooks

- Scissors.

Instructions

1. First, you must tie cotton twine around each end of each dowel and then hang it from the hooks above your door. Create a lark's head knot with your first 16-foot strand of rope by folding it in half and placing it over your dowel. Using a lark's head knot, add each 16-foot strand of rope until you have 22 strands. This will provide you with 44 strands you can use in your work.

2. Drape the end of the outer center rope over your door hook by pulling it across the front in every one of the other ropes to the left. This will serve as the foundation for the following set of knots, which will be called a half-hitch and produce a horizontal row.

3. Make a simple knot in the rope you just stretched across using the second strand from the right side. Position the knot so that it is approximately 6 inches below the dowel.

4. Using the same strand, make a second tie over the first strand used as the base. This type of knot is known as a half-hitch knot. The fifth step is to check that they are level and consistent throughout. Repeat with the third, second, and fourth ropes from the outside, and tie additional half-hitch knots to be as tight as possible. You'll start to recognize the recurring theme.

5. This is a half-hitch that runs horizontally. Proceed to tie successive ropes in only one knot until you have reached the end of the strand. It is not desirable for this to feel so snug that it brings the breadth around the edges.

6. Beginning on the appropriate side again, use the four strands furthest from the center to tie a square knot approximately 1.5 inches below the line of knots you created in Step Seven. Look at this macrame stockings post for further explanation on tying a square knot. After skipping the five through eight strands, tie a final square knot with the nine through twelve strands.

7. You should continue skipping four and then tying four until you have reached the end of the row. Beginning once more on the right side, take the four strands that you omitted (five through eight), and use them to tie a square knot approximately three inches below the dowel. The tenth step is to continue making square knots with the groups of four strands skipped until you have completed that row.

8. Pull apart the two outermost strands on the right side and set them to the side. Then, using strands three through six, build another square knot approximately 11 inches below the row of horizontal knots created in step seven. After that, create a second square knot with the afterward four strands about 1.5 inches higher than the last squared knot. The remaining two strands will not be utilized in any way by you.

9. Beginning on the right side again, make another row of lateral half-hitch knots by repeatedly performing steps three through seven. Beginning on the left side, using the same foundation strand of rope, make another row of horizontal half-hitch knots about 2.5 inches below the prior one. In this case, you should begin on the left and work your way to the right.

10. construct a row of square knots on every left side, avoiding skipping strands. This row should rest approximately 1 inch below the line of horizontal knots you just made. After that, make a further row with square knots by bypassing the first six strands on the right and left after tying a full line of square knots. This will generate a third row of square knots.

11. One might refer to this as an alternation square knot. There mustn't be a lot of space amongst these rows to bring them closer together when you add every square knot. Carry on working until they have approximately thirteen rows of consecutive square knots because this piece is the center of your table runner, everything that comes after it will reflect what you have previously woven in the portion above it.

12. Add another row of knots to the horizontal half-hitch row, beginning at the outer left side and moving to the right. Move up about 2.5 inches and form another horizontal row of half-hitch knots that proceed from right to left using the same foundation rope.

13. This row should move opposite to the previous row. For this part of the process, you will need to leave the two pieces of rope that are furthest to the right untied and proceed to tie the square knot with strands two through six of the rope. If you want to make another square knot, skip strands seventh through ten and work with strands 11 through 14. Repeat the process so that you skip every fourth strand of the yarn. On the left side, there will be six strands for you to work with.

14. On the left side, skip rows of one and two, then tie strands three to six into a rectangular knot about 1.5 inches below the row containing the last line of square knots.

The subsequent four strands should be skipped, and the pattern for the second row of eight square knots should be completed afterward. Because of this, you will now have an additional six strands on the opposite side.

15. Measure 11 inches down from the most recent row of horizontal knots, then use the four strands from the right side that are furthest out to tie a square knot. After that, tie a square knot with the following four strands about 1.5 inches above the previous knot. Repeat the above until you have completed the entire row. Finally, about 1.5 inches below each pair of alternating square knots, tie one final row of diagonal half-hitch knots.

16. You can trim the ends as long or as short as you like but keep track of the length on the other end. Take the cotton twine off your dowel, and then use your fingers to untie each lark's head knot. The lark's head knot loop should then have its center cut out, and the ends should be trimmed.

6.3: Backdrop

Supplies

- S-hooks

- Picture rail

- Rope

Instructions

1. Briefly, lengths of rope should be tied and secured to the pole to denote the locations of the three portions.

2. You should have an excess of at least 40 centimeters (15 34") on either end. You will need to cut 40 lengths of rope measuring 3 meters (11818 inches) each; you will use 20 of these lengths for each of the 30-centimeter (1178-inch) pieces that makeup parts one and three.

3. Attach 20 lengths to part one using Lark's head knots and attach 20 lengths to section three using Lark's head knots.

4. Remove two lengths of rope measuring 5 meters (1957.8 inches). Fold each of them in half so that one side lengths 1 meter (393/8 inches), and the other measures 4 meters (15712 inches).

5. When tying the lengths on either side from the marker that separates portions one and two with a lark's head knot, be sure that the two lower extremities of these two measures are facing one another so that they become involved in the heart of the knot.

6. After you have completed this procedure for the second section marker, work ten half-square knots into each of the freshly knotted lengths. Remove 40 lengths of rope measuring 3 meters (11818 inches).

7. Each one should be folded in half, and then a lark's head knot should be used to link it to part two. Make one row of squared knots on part two by working from left to center for each row. Before beginning the following row, you should untangle the first two strands at the beginning of the second row.

8. After this row, two strands should be left behind for you to work with. Continue working your way down in rows, reducing by two strings at each end until you have 20 rows of squared knots. Now continue Step 6 for portions one and three. The first line will have ten square knots, and the number of knots in each subsequent row will decrease by one.

9. When you have finished working through each part completely, you will have four strands remaining. To make a triangle, finish two rows of diagonal clove hitches knots in each of the three sections by working towards the outside in each section inwards the middle.

10. When you have reached the end, begin tying a series of half-square cube knots using the four strands in the middle of each triangle. Continue doing this until you have reached the desired length. Perform a wrap knot to secure the two ends together. Now complete the quarter square knots separating each segment by working them to the desired length.

10. A wrap knot should be used to secure the ends. Remove three strands of rope measuring 2 meters (7834"). After folding each piece in half lengthwise, use lark's head knots to secure the strands within the openings in the middle of section two. Make two plaits slightly longer than 50 centimeters (1934 inches) each and divide into two groups of three.

11. At the intersection of the rows of four clove hitch knots, the plaited strands should be crossed, and their ends inserted into the spaces between sections one and three. Tie a knot in the back to keep it in place and finish it off. You will need to cut four strands of rope that are 5 meters long (1957.8 inches), then tie a lark's head knot to connect two strands on the two ends of the piece.

12. Again, the folding ratio is 1-meter (39.3/8 inches) to 4 meters (15712 inches), with the 1-meter (39.3/8 inches) lengths on the inside. With each length of rope, tie approximately one meter (39 3/8 inches) worth of half square knots. After ensuring that the length of both sides is the same, bring the ends closer to the center, and then push them through the hole in section two that is created where the line of clove half knot knots meet. First, secure it by tying it in the back, then cut it.

13. For additional texture, add evenly spaced plaits across all sections. Use the primary image as a guide to ensure the plants are the same on both sides of the section. To portions one and three, please add six plaits each, and to section two, please add eight plaits.

6.4: Macramé Bouquet Wraps

Supplies

- Macramé cord or ribbon

- Beads, flowers, feathers, or other embellishments (optional)

- Scissors

Instructions

- Measure the length of the macramé cord or ribbon you'll need to wrap around your bouquet.

- Add a few extra inches for tying knots and securing the wrap.

- Fold the cord or ribbon in half and place it under the base of your bouquet.

- Bring the two ends of the cord or ribbon up and cross them over each other.

- Take the left end over the right end and pass it through the loop created by the right end.

- Pull both ends tight to create a knot at the base of your bouquet.

- Repeat these steps to create another knot, ensuring it is secure.

- Continue knotting the cord or ribbon around the base of your bouquet, alternating between left-over-right and right-over-left knots.

- As you knot, you can incorporate beads, flowers, feathers, or other embellishments by sliding them onto the cord or ribbon before tying the knots.

- Continue knotting and adding embellishments until you reach the desired length of the wrap.

- Once you've reached the end, tie a secure knot to finish the wrap.

- Trim any excess cord or ribbon, leaving a small tail for a clean finish.

6.5: Macramé Chair Decorations

Supplies

- Macramé cord or rope

- Scissors

Instructions

- Measure the length of macramé cord or rope you'll need to drape across the chair back and secure it in place.

- Cut two pieces of cord or rope to the desired length, ensuring they are equal in length.

- Take one piece of cord or rope and fold it in half.

- Place the folded section of the cord or rope over the top of the chair back, with the looped end facing down.

- Bring the loose ends of the cord or rope through the loop and pull them tight to secure the cord or rope to the chair back.

- Repeat these steps with the second piece of cord or rope, placing it slightly below the first piece to create a layered effect.

- Adjust the length and positioning of the cords or ropes to achieve the desired look.

- Optional: Add decorative knots, braids, or fringe to the cords or ropes to enhance the design.

- Repeat the process for each chair you want to decorate.

- Once all the cords or ropes are in place, make sure they are secure and adjust them as needed.

- Trim any excess cord or rope for a neat finish.

Chapter 7: Macramé for Fashion Accessories

7.1: Creating macramé belts

Supplies

You will need the following materials to build a macrame belt:

- Paton's 100% mercerized cotton, 4ply.

- 50 x 6mm wooden beads with 1.5mm holes

- Map pins,

- a macramé board,

- a darning needle, and

- little scissors

- 2.5 x 130cm (1 x 5114 in) in size

Instructions

1. To locate the midpoint, fold 16 x 3.5m pieces of yarn in half. At the top of your macramé board, insert four lengths through each of the 4 center slots. Onto each of the middle four ropes, thread a bead. Separate the cables coming through the bead, then tuck two into the side slots to form a right angle.

2. Take the initial right-hand chord from the center, going under and over the diagonal cords before coming back down along the left side for the vertical cable. Pull the string tight to tie a half hitch knot and then continue with another section of the same cord. Repeat these two steps with each of the other right cables in turn.

3. Take the cable from underneath the diagonal cords, cross it across, and then position it again under the vertical chord on the right side. Repeat the operation on the left. To tie the knot, tighten the string and wrap it around one more. To make two diagonal ribs, repeat on both cords on the left side.

4. Move the four ropes on each side to make working with the rectangular knots easier. Cross the left cords across the right cord while working on all four cables. Pass the right cable through the left loop and over the two "core cords" in the center.

5. Take the opposite cord over a left cord and beneath the two centers' "core cords" to finish the square knot. Take the left cord and pass it through the right loop and the two "core cords" in the center. Separate the center eight cords for the subsequent row and tie two rectangular knots on each side. Separate the center four cords for the final row and tie a square knot. Additionally, tie a square tie on either side. Work a row of two square knots and a single square tie in the center to complete the diamond-shaped form.

6. Place a map pin on each side at the tip of the rib. The space on your macramé boards below the one you had on the right is where you should hide the left pair or diagonal cords after taking them across. Work half-hitches from the outside cords into the center. Repeat the rib by inserting the right diagonal cords into the left slot.

7. Repeat steps 2 and 3 until the macramé is half the desired length. At this point, you may add the next bead color to the center of four strands. The macramé stitch from the center bead should be repeated as you turn the belt around. After trimming the tails, attach beads to pairs and threads. Finish by making an overhand knot with each pair of cords.

7.2: Headband

Materials

- 4mm GANXXET Soft Linen Rope with Zero Waste, One Strand

- comb

- incisive scissors

- the clipboard

- Measurement tape

- wood dowel

- fabric adhesive

- the headband

Notes

- requires familiarity with the square knot, larks head knot, and diagonal clove hitch knot.

- Easiest to create with a clipboard and a level surface.

- There are four diamonds throughout the whole pattern.

- Square Knot with Diagonal Clove Knot

- A rope is tied around and guided to make elaborate patterns using the "Lead Rope."

- three parts at 55"

Instructions

1. Apply a "larks head knot" on the wooden dowel to secure all the parts.

2. Attach to the clipboard.

3. Primary Diamond Shape

4. Make a Square Knot using the four ropes closest to the center.

5. Your "lead rope" should be the third rope from the left. The top of the first diamond is made by pulling the rope at an angle downward and to the left.

6. Utilize the second rope from your left and fasten it to the "lead rope" Repeat the "Clove Hitch Knot" for two CHKs.

7. Repeat two CHKs with the first rope from the left.

8. Repeat the same on the right side to make the top of our first diamond shape.

9. Pull the rope at an angle downhill to the right using the third rope coming from the left as the "lead rope."

10. Utilizing the second rope from the right, tie a "Clove Hitch Knot" and link it to the "lead rope" twice more.

11. Repeat two CHKs with the first rope from the right.

12. By using 4 center ropes, tie a beautiful center knot.

13. Separate into right and left parts of two ropes.

14. Cross the right side of the left.

15. Pick the appropriate side. To tie a basic knot, fold the left section over and under.

16. Tighten and lift.

17. complete the diamond's bottom left side.

18. Use the first rope on all left as your "lead rope" and pull the other ropes at an angle rightward.

19. Use the leftmost rope to connect to the lead rope. apply CHK 2x's.

20. Connect the lead rope with the third rope from the left. apply CHK 2x's.

21. Pull the side ropes.

22. Use the lead rope from the first rope on the opposite side to complete the bottom of the opposite side of the diamond by pulling the rope at an angle to the left.

23. Use the second rope from the right, join it to the lead rope, and then use CHK 2x's.

24. Use the third rope from the right, then use CHK 2x's to link it to the lead rope.

25. Using the second rope from the left, connect to the lead rope with two CHKs while keeping the opposite lead rope in your left hand and angling it downward to your left to cross over the left lead rope.

26. Utilize the first rope on the left and secure it to the lead rope using 2 CHK's first diamond shape. Yay!

27. To make a total number of 3 diamonds, repeat the procedure above.

28. Make a square knot out of the last diamond.

29. Take a piece out of the wooden dowel.

30. Trim the piece leaving a half-inch of fringe.

31. Brush out the fringe with your comb and trim it again.

32. Find the headband's center.

33. Place macramé slightly out of alignment or whatever you choose.

34. Apply your adhesive straight on the headband.

35. *TIP* Measure your piece's length and make the glue line the same length.

36. Apply pressure to the headband to secure the macrame.

37. Dry the glue.

38. Enjoy!

7.3: Handbag

Supplies

- One set of circular wooden handles

- Mustard 3mm linen cord

- scissors

- yardstick

Instructions

- Step One: Cut 32 11' cotton cord lengths.

- Step Two: Tie 16 strands to every handle with a lark's head knot. Fold the strand in two and fold it in half from one handle's outward rounded section to the back to make a lark's head knot. Pull the two open ends towards the folded middle. Result: Lark's knot.

- Step Three: Repeat sixteen strands on each handle. Avoid visual disruption by placing all knots on the same edge of the handle.

- Step Four: Use the first four rope strands on the left edge of one handle to start the initial set of square knots. To simplify, shift the other strands to the side.

- Step Five: Wrap the initial strand over both subsequent strands underneath the fourth to form a "4".

- Step Six: Fold the final strand under both previous strands and over the first strand bend. It resembles an inverted heart. Tighten the outside two strands. A half-knot.

- Step Seven: Reverse the outer rope overlap sequence to make another half knot. The right outer rope goes over the middle two ropes but beneath the left outer rope. Then the left outer rope will travel behind the central two ropes and emerge over the curve in the outer left rope.

- Step Eight: Make another square knot with the following four strands.

- Step Nine: Alternating square knots on the second row. Use the initial eight left-side strands. To work with the four center strands, skip the initial two on the left and the final two on the right.

- Step Ten: Knot the four strands into a square.

- Step Eleven: Make a square knot with the two right-side remaining strands and the following two.

- Step 12: Looks good. Keep knotting this second row. Add a third row of round knots, an additional row of alternating tangles, a fifth, and a sixth row.

- Step Thirteen: duplicate steps 4–12 on the second handle.

- Fourteen: Align the handles. Make sure that the handles are right-side up. Make an alternate square knot with two strands from each side.

- Step Fifteen: Finish that row by tying a square knot from center to edge, except for the final two or four threads on either end. Start spacing rows after the ninth row. This expands your bag's bottom half.

- Step Sixteen: Fold the bag in half with the incorrect sides, with the handles facing each other after fifteen rows. Finish the rows by knotting the bag's open sides.

- Step Seventeen: The top knots are more closely spaced than the bottom.

- Step Eighteen: This bag may have fringe on the bottom or inside. If you want everything tucked inside like mine, flip your purse inside out without the right handles opposite each other.

- Step Nineteen: Tie the twine from the bag's front to its rear.

- Step 20: Take each strand from a single knot on the leading side and one from a close knot on the rear side and tie them together snugly.

- Step 21: Double knot. Follow along till all strands are double-knotted.

- Twenty-Two: Evenly trim your strands.

- Step Twenty-Three: Comb your strands to make them full if you keep them outside your bag.

7.4: Macramé Hair Clips

Supplies

- 4mm macramé cord

- Hair clips

- Scissors

Instructions

- Cut two strands of macramé cord, each twice the length of the hair clip.

- Fold one cord in half and attach it to the hair clip using a lark's head knot. Repeat this step with the second cord on the opposite side of the hair clip.

- Divide the cords into four sections, with two cords in each section.

- Start creating square knots by taking the two outer cords from one section and tying them over the two inner cords using a right-hand square knot. Repeat this step for each section.

- Continue tying square knots until you reach the desired length of the hair clip. You can add beads or incorporate different knot variations to create patterns.

- Once you reach the end, tie off the cords with an overhand knot and trim any excess cord.

7.5: Macramé Scrunchies

Supplies

- 4mm macramé cord

- Elastic hair tie

- Scissors

Instructions

- Measure and cut several strands of macramé cord, each approximately three times the length of the hair tie.

- Fold one cord in half and place it under the hair tie, forming a loop.

- Take the ends of the cord and pull them through the loop, creating a lark's head knot around the hair tie.

- Repeat steps 2 and 3 with the remaining cords, spacing them evenly around the hair tie.

- Once all the cords are attached, start tying square knots by pairing up two adjacent cords and tying them over the remaining cords using right-hand square knots.

- Continue tying square knots until you cover the entire hair tie with macramé.

- When you reach the end, tie off the cords with an overhand knot and trim any excess cord.

7.6: Macramé Bag Charm

Supplies

- 4mm macramé cord

- Keychain or lobster clasp

- Beads or charms (optional)

- Scissors

Instructions

- Cut a long strand of macramé cord, approximately four times the desired length of the bag charm.

- Fold the cord in half and attach it to the keychain or lobster clasp using a lark's head knot. Divide the cord into four sections, with two strands in each section.

- Start creating square knots by taking the two outer strands from one section and tying them over the two inner strands using a right-hand square knot. Repeat this step for each section.

- Continue tying square knots until you reach the desired length of the bag charm. You can add beads or charms along the way for added decoration.

- Once you reach the end, tie off the cords with an overhand knot and trim any excess cord.

7.7: Macramé Sunglasses Strap

Supplies

- 4mm macramé cord

- Sunglasses

- Scissors

Instructions

- Measure and cut two long strands of macramé cord, each approximately three times the desired length of the sunglasses strap.

- Fold one cord in half and attach it to one end of the sunglasses using a lark's head knot. Repeat this step with the second cord on the opposite end of the sunglasses.

- Divide each cord into two sections, with one strand in each section.

- Start creating square knots by taking the two outer strands from one section and tying them over the two inner strands using a right-hand square knot. Repeat this step for each section.

- Continue tying square knots until you reach the desired length of the sunglasses strap.

- You can add beads or incorporate different knot variations for added style.

- Once you reach the end, tie off the cords with an overhand knot and trim any excess cord.

7.8: Macramé Hat Band

Supplies

- 4mm macramé cord

- Hat

- Scissors

Instructions

- Measure and cut a long strand of macramé cord, approximately twice the circumference of the hat.

- Attach one end of the cord to the hat by tying a lark's head knot.

- Divide the cord into four sections, with one strand in each section.

- Start creating square knots by taking the two outer strands from one section and tying them over the two inner strands using a right-hand square knot. Repeat this step for each section.

- Continue tying square knots until you reach the desired length of the hat band. You can add beads or incorporate different knot variations for decorative accents.

- Once you reach the end, tie off the cord with an overhand knot and trim any excess cord.

7.9: Macramé Phone Case

Supplies

- 3mm cotton cord

- Scissors

- Tape measure or ruler

- Small beads (optional)

- Button or snap closure (optional)

Instructions

- Measure and cut 8 pieces of cotton cord, each measuring 2 times the length of your phone plus a few extra inches for knots.

- Fold all 8 cords in half and align the ends. This will create 16 cords.

- Create a loop at the folded end of the cords and secure it to a surface using tape or a clip.

- Separate the cords into groups of 4 and start creating square knots:

- Take the left cord of the first group and cross it over the two middle cords. Then, take the right cord and pass it over the left cord and under the two middle cords, coming out through the loop created by the left cord.

- Pull the cords tight to create a square knot. Repeat this process with the remaining cords. Continue making square knots until you have the desired length for the bottom part of the phone case.

- Once you have reached the desired length, gather all the cords together and create another row of square knots to close the bottom part.

- After closing the bottom, continue making square knots for the sides of the phone case.

- You can make it as tall as you want, leaving enough space at the top to accommodate the phone.

- Once you have reached the desired height, tie all the cords together at the top with a knot

- Optional: Add beads to the cords for decoration. You can slide them onto the cords before making knots.

- To create a closure, you can either attach a button or sew on a snap closure to secure the top of the phone case.

7.10: Macramé Wallet or Coin Purse

Supplies

- 3mm cotton cord

- Scissors

- Tape measure or ruler

- Button or snap closure

- Needle and thread (if using a button closure)

Instructions

- Measure and cut 8 pieces of cotton cord, each measuring the desired length of your wallet or coin purse plus a few extra inches for knots.

- Fold all 8 cords in half and align the ends. This will create 16 cords.

- Create a loop at the folded end of the cords and secure it to a surface using tape or a clip.

- Separate the cords into groups of 4 and start creating square knots, just like in the phone case instructions. Make a bottom base of square knots, leaving an opening at the center for the wallet or coin purse.

- Once you have the desired length for the bottom base, continue making square knots for the sides of the wallet or coin purse. Make it as tall as you want, leaving enough space for the closure.

- After reaching the desired height, tie all the cords together at the top with a knot. Attach a button or sew on a snap closure to secure the top of the wallet or coin purse.

- Optional: You can create compartments inside the wallet or coin purse by attaching additional cords and creating dividers with square knots.

Chapter 8: Macramé for Kids and Teens

Macrame for Kids is a unique collection of patterns for young people interested in learning more about this craft. The following list of Macrame projects features a variety of finished goods, such as jewelry, key chains, animals, and decorations. Macrame is an activity that the whole family might enjoy doing together. These patterns are versatile enough for a night of crafting with the kids, a youth club, or even an art lesson at school.

8.1: Fun and Age-Appropriate Macramé Projects for Children and Teenagers

The patterns are beginner-friendly macramé crafts that adults can complete. The patterns are straightforward and call for a comparatively small amount of fabric. Therefore, before going on to more difficult projects, try one or two simpler ones first. One of the first kinds of craft I can recall being familiarized with was Macrame.

They practically define for me what crafting can be about doing a project that isn't too tough but looks very cool and can also be extremely useful. Macrame crafts have always been my favorite type of craft. You may also utilize macrame crafts to construct unique clothing accessories or pieces of hippie costuming for Halloween. Examples of these include headbands and bracelets. Children might begin by making friendship bracelets for their classmates, keychains, and room decorations.

8.2: Keychains

Here are step-by-step instructions for the keychain.

Supplies

- Colored embroidery thread or macramé cord

- Scissors

- A ring for a keychain

Instructions

1. Attach the ring to the keychain in the second step. Make a crease down the middle of the key ring or splits ring you have.

2. Create a lark's skull knot by passing the folded end of each of your cords through the loop that forms another of your cords. To prevent the ring from moving once it is in place, pull the string until it is taut.

3. Organize the wires and cords. If you have more than one cord, lay them all out parallel. You can give the whole thing the same color or use assorted colors to create a livelier pattern.

4. Proceed to Step 4 to start tying the knots. Create a loop in the other cords by taking the first cable from the left and bringing it onto the other cords. Move the tail end of the right cable over the end of the left cord, then pass it through the loop that has been produced. To make the knot more secure, pull on both ends. This type of knot is known as a square knot.

5. Perform the tying process one more. Carry on forming square knots with identical ropes that are on the outside. Take the left wire and loop around the other cords with it. Then, pass the right cord over the tail attached to the left cord before passing it through the loop. To make it tighter, pull it. Repeat these steps as often as necessary until your keychain is the appropriate length.

6. Beads can be added in Step 6 (optional). If you want your keychain to have beads, slide them onto the center cords before making each square knot. As you work to tighten the knots, the beads will remain in their current position.

7. Putting the final changes on the keychain. Collect all the cords once you have achieved the necessary length. Finish up by tying a knot but leave a little loop at the end to attach keys. Remove any excess cord that is longer than the knot.

8.3: Macramé Wall Hanging for Kids' Room

Supplies

- Macramé cord in various colors

- Wooden dowel or branch

- Scissors

- Optional: beads, feathers, or other decorations

Instructions

- Cut several strands of macramé cord in different colors. The number of strands will depend on the size and design you want for your wall hanging.

- Fold each cord in half and attach them to the wooden dowel using a lark's head knot. Repeat this step with all the cords, spacing them evenly across the dowel.

- Arrange the cords in the desired pattern. You can create simple vertical or diagonal lines, or experiment with more intricate designs like chevrons or feathers.

- Once you're happy with the arrangement, it's time to start knotting. You can use various macramé knots like square knots, half square knots, or spiral knots to create texture and interest.

- Follow the pattern of your choice, knotting the cords together and creating a series of knots along the length of the wall hanging. You can alternate colors, mix different knot styles, or add beads between the knots for extra decoration.

- Continue knotting until you reach the desired length for your wall hanging. Make sure to leave enough space at the bottom to create a decorative fringe.

- Once you've finished knotting, trim the ends of the cords to create a straight edge at the bottom.

- To add a fringe, cut additional strands of cord in the same or contrasting colors. Attach them to the bottom of the wall hanging using a lark's head knot. Trim the fringe to your desired length.

- Optional: You can further embellish the wall hanging by adding beads, feathers, or other decorations. Attach them to the cords using knots or by threading them onto the cords before knotting.

- Once you're satisfied with the design, trim any excess cord at the top of the wall hanging to create an even edge.

- Hang your macramé wall hanging in the child's room using a nail or hook, and enjoy the colorful and unique addition to their space.

8.4: Macramé Feather Bookmark

Supplies

- Macramé cord in a color of your choice

- Scissors

- Wooden or metal bookmark base

- Craft glue

Instructions

- Cut a length of macramé cord, around 1 yard long, to create the feather design. Fold the cord in half and place it over the bookmark base, with the looped end facing downward.

- Bring the loose ends of the cord through the looped end, creating a lark's head knot around the bookmark base. This will secure the cord in place.

- Divide the cord into three equal sections, with two outer sections and a center section.

- To create the feather shape, start by making double half hitch knots. Take the left outer section and bring it over the center section, then pass it under the right outer section. Pull it through the loop created and tighten the knot.

- Repeat the double half hitch knot with the right outer section, bringing it over the center section and under the left outer section. Pull it through the loop and tighten the knot.

- Continue alternating between the left and right outer sections, creating double half hitch knots until you reach the desired length for the feather.

- Once you've reached the desired length, secure the cord by tying a knot at the end.

- Trim any excess cord, leaving a small tail at the end for a decorative touch.

- Optional: You can further embellish the feather by adding small beads or charms. Thread them onto the cords before creating the double half hitch knots.

- Apply a small amount of craft glue to the back of the macramé feather to secure any loose ends and ensure its durability.

- Allow the glue to dry completely before using the bookmark.

8.5: Rainbow Dreamcatcher

Supplies

- 1 metal hoop (medium-sized)

- Colored cotton cord in various rainbow colors

- White yarn or cotton threads

- Decorative beads

- Tape or pins

- Scissors

- Optional: Smaller hoop

- Optional: Colored feathers

Instructions

- Prepare your metal hoop and ensure it is clean and free of rust. You can also use a smaller hoop as a base to create a more intricate design.

- Cut the colored cotton cord into different lengths, depending on the desired size of your rainbow dreamcatcher. You can choose any combination of colors you like.

- Attach the colored cotton cords to the metal hoop using a basic knot. Make sure they are securely fastened.

- Divide the cords into groups based on color and create a diagonal pattern by tying square knots. Start with the first group of cords on the left side and continue across to the right side. Repeat this pattern until you have completed the rainbow shape.

- Once you have reached the end of the rainbow, continue with a section of white yarn or cotton threads. This will represent the clouds beneath the rainbow.

- To add decorative elements, thread colorful beads onto some of the cords and secure them with knots. You can also attach colored feathers to the bottom of the dreamcatcher for added flair.

- Trim any excess cords to create a clean and neat finish.

- Optional: Attach a smaller hoop to the top of the dreamcatcher using cords or yarn, creating a loop for hanging.

- Hang your rainbow dreamcatcher in a special place where it can catch dreams and bring colorful vibes to any room.

- Note: Feel free to experiment with different colors, patterns, and embellishments to make your rainbow dreamcatcher unique and personal.

8.6: Macramé Toy Hanger

Supplies

- Macramé cord in a color of your choice

- Wooden dowel or metal ring

- Scissors

- Hooks or rings for hanging

Instructions

- Cut the macramé cord into different lengths, depending on how many levels you want to create in your toy hanger. Make sure you have enough cord for each level.

- Take one piece of cord and fold it in half. Pass the folded end through the wooden dowel or metal ring and pull the ends through the loop to create a lark's head knot around the dowel or ring.

- Repeat this step with the other pieces of cord, making sure to evenly distribute them along the dowel or ring.

- Once all the cords are attached, create square knots with adjacent cord pairs. Take two neighboring cords and cross the left cord over the right cord. Then pass the left cord under the right cord and through the loop created. Pull both cords to tighten the knot. Repeat this process with the next cord pairs.

- Continue creating square knots along each level of the hanger, alternating between adjacent cord pairs. You can vary the pattern by using different knot variations or adding beads for decoration.

- Once you have reached the desired length for your toy hanger, tie a secure knot at the bottom to hold all the cords together.

- Attach hooks or rings to the top of the dowel or ring for hanging the toy hanger.

- Hang the toy hanger in a suitable location and use it to display your children's favorite toys.

8.7: Macramé Headphone Cord Organizer

Supplies

- Macramé cord in a color of your choice

- Scissors

- Keyring or small carabiner

Instructions

- Cut a length of macramé cord, approximately 90 cm long, to serve as the base for your headphone cord organizer.

- Fold the cord in half and attach it to the keyring or small carabiner using a lark's head knot. This will create a loop at the top of your organizer.

- Divide the cord into two equal halves and begin creating square knots. Take the left cord and cross it over the right cord, then bring it under the right cord and through the loop created. Pull both cords to tighten the knot. Repeat this process with the next cord pair.

- Continue creating square knots until you reach your desired length. You can add beads or charms to the cords as desired for additional decoration.

- Once you've reached the desired length, tie a knot at the end to secure the cords in place.

- Trim any excess cord, leaving a small tail at the end.

- Attach your headphone cords to the loops created by the macramé knots. Wrap the cords around the organizer and secure them in place by tucking the ends through the loops.

- Your macramé headphone cord organizer is now ready to use. Hang it from your bag, backpack, or keyring to keep your headphone cords organized and easily accessible.

8.8: Friendship Bracelet with Macramé Beads

Supplies

- 3 colors of macramé cord (each about 90cm long)

- Scissors

- Small wooden beads (assorted colors)

- Clear craft glue

- Clipboard or tape to secure your work

Instructions

- Start by cutting the three cords into equal lengths.

- Fold the cords in half and create a loop at the top, securing them to a clipboard or with tape.

- Arrange the cords in color order from left to right (e.g., blue, green, pink).

- Take the first cord (blue) and make a forward knot over the two neighboring cords (green and pink).

- Repeat this process with the blue cord, making a forward knot over the green and pink cords. Continue making forward knots with the blue cord until it reaches the right edge.

- Repeat these steps with the green and pink cords.

- After completing several rows of forward knots, you can add wooden beads to the bracelet.

- Slide a wooden bead onto one of the cords before making a forward knot with that cord. Repeat this process, adding beads at desired intervals along the bracelet.

- Continue making forward knots and adding beads until you reach the desired length. Once you've reached the desired length, tie a knot at the end of the bracelet to secure the cords.

- Trim any excess cord and use clear craft glue to secure the knots and prevent unraveling.

- Allow the glue to dry completely before wearing or gifting the friendship bracelet.

8.9: Macramé Feather Earrings

These macramé feather earrings make a stylish and unique accessory for teenagers. You can experiment with different cord colors and lengths to create your own personalized designs.

Supplies

- 3mm macramé cord (assorted colors)

- Earring hooks

- Scissors

- Comb or brush

Instructions

- Cut two pieces of macramé cord, each about 10 inches long.

- Fold one piece of cord in half and attach it to a sturdy surface using a clip or tape. This will be the base of your feather.

- Take the second piece of cord and fold it in half, then attach it to the base cord using a lark's head knot.

- Separate the four strands of cord into pairs and start making square knots about 2 inches below the base.

- Continue making square knots until you reach the desired length for your feather. You can vary the length of the cords to create a feather-like shape.

- Once you've reached the desired length, trim the ends of the cords to create a pointed shape resembling a feather.

- Repeat the same steps to create a second feather.

- Attach an earring hook to the top of each feather by opening the hook and sliding it onto the base cord.

- Secure the earring hook by closing it.

- Repeat the entire process to create a matching pair of macramé feather earrings.

8.10: Macramé Wall Hanging with Personalized Name

Supplies

- Macramé cord in a color of your choice

- Wooden dowel or branch

- Scissors

- Craft glue

- Letter beads or wooden alphabet beads

- Optional: additional decorative elements such as feathers or pom poms

Instructions

- Cut several lengths of macramé cord, each approximately 90cm long, depending on the desired length of the wall hanging.

- Fold each cord in half and attach them to the wooden dowel or branch using a lark's head knot. Space the cords evenly along the dowel or branch.

- Once all the cords are attached, separate them into pairs.

- Starting from the left side, take two adjacent cords and tie a square knot by crossing the left cord over the right cord and then passing it under the right cord and through the loop created. Pull both cords to tighten the knot. Repeat this process with the next pair of cords.

- Continue tying square knots across the row, making sure to maintain the same pattern and tension. This will create a series of diagonal lines in the macramé design.

- After completing the first row, move to the second row and repeat the process. You can vary the pattern by starting with the opposite diagonal direction.

- Once you've reached the desired length for the wall hanging, it's time to personalize it with the child's name. Thread the letter beads or wooden alphabet beads onto the individual cords, spelling out the name. You can add decorative elements such as feathers or pom poms between the letters for added flair.

- Secure the beads and decorative elements in place by tying knots below and above each one.

- Trim any excess cord below the knots, leaving a small tail for a decorative touch.

- Optional: You can add additional fringes or tassels at the bottom of the wall hanging for added texture and visual interest.

- Apply a small amount of craft glue to the knots and tails to secure them in place and prevent unraveling.

- Allow the glue to dry completely before hanging the personalized macramé wall hanging in the room.

Chapter 9: Macramé for Pet Accessories

9.1: Pet Collar

Supplies

- 2x 3ply 5mm Linen Rope

- 1" side-release buckle

- 3/4" D-ring scissors

- Tape

Instructions

1. Cut two 120" 5mm 3ply cotton ropes. Cut a 15-inch third rope. This 15" rope will be saved for the last stage.

2. Next, join one end of your two 120" ropes. Insert the ends through one buckle side. Draw these ends simultaneously to draw 25" of rope through the buckle. These are your filler ropes. Working ropes are the longer lengths of rope put on each side of the filler ropes. Working ropes are 95" long.

3. Tape your seatbelt to a desk or tabletop. Use paint-safe tape! Masking, painters, and washi tape work well.

4. Start typing! Separate your ropes first. Your two fillers ropes will run down the center, and you'll be using ropes to both left and right.

5. First, lay your left work rope horizontally over the filler ropes. Place the right work line directly over the top of the left. Ropes create a 4.

6. To tie the knot, the right working line must pass behind the extra ropes and via the left-side gap. Tighten the knot by pulling your left and left working ropes away from their filler ropes.

7. Square knot step two. We'll reverse it. Place your right work rope horizontally over the filler ropes. The left work rope will go over the right.

8. D ring after 2 square knots above the buckle. Pull both fill ropes around your D rings so it's against the pair of square knots above the buckle.

9. D ring after 2 knots that are square below the buckle. Pull the 2 fill ropes through the D ring so it's against the pair of square knots beneath the buckle.

10. Alternate "4" and "P" knots for the rest of the dog collar.

11. Square knots till 18" in length. In this phase, you may adjust your dog's neck size by adding or removing knots.

12. Untie each rope end knot. Add the second buckle end to the rope-attached buckle.

13. Pull all four ends (filler and subsequent ropes) over the top of the clasp and leave a 3" gap between the clasp and the last round knot.

14. Separate the buckle's ends and tape the fresh buckle side flat. One-square knot the buckle.

15. Gather the rope ends in front within the 3" space. Working ropes are usually longer than filler ropes.

16. The smaller 15" rope from the first step will wrap the 3" gap. To tie the wrapping knot, insert the short 15" rope at the exact center of your collars with a 1" tail straight up over the buckle.

17. Next, loop the rope end to form a lowercase d.

18. Pull the end through your loop after wrapping the rope to fill the 3" space.

19. To secure the tying knot, carefully draw upwards on the top of the 1" tail.

20. Pull the loop into the wrapped knot and cut the top rope.

21. Your wrapping knot may have leftover ropes. Option 1: Trim ropes to 2" and unravel for a charming fringe feature. Option 2: trim ropes flush with the wrapping knot.

9.2: Pet Bed

Supplies

- 60m of 6mm cotton rope

- Scissors

- Round cushion or pillow insert

- Tape measure

- Tape

Instructions

- Start by measuring the diameter of your round cushion or pillow insert. This will determine the size of the pet bed.

- Cut 8 equal lengths of rope, each measuring twice the diameter of your cushion.

- Take one rope and fold it in half. This will be your center rope.

- Position the center rope vertically, with the folded end at the top.

- Take two more ropes and place them horizontally across the center rope, forming a cross shape. Secure the ropes in place by tying an overhand knot at the center.

- Now you will start creating the spiral pattern for the pet bed. Take one of the remaining ropes and place it diagonally across the horizontal ropes, going under the center rope and over the other horizontal rope. Secure it in place with an overhand knot.

- Repeat this step with the remaining ropes, alternating the direction of the diagonal ropes (some going from left to right, others from right to left), and creating a spiral pattern around the center.

- Continue adding ropes and knotting them in a spiral pattern until you reach the desired size for the pet bed. Make sure to keep the tension even throughout the process. Once you've reached the desired size, tie off the ends of the ropes with an overhand knot to secure the bed.

- Place the round cushion or pillow insert in the center of the macramé bed. If desired, you can add decorative touches such as tassels or fringe to the edges of the bed.

- Your pet bed is now ready for your furry friend to enjoy!

- Remember to double-check the size of the bed to ensure it will comfortably accommodate your pet. You can also adjust the size of the ropes and the number of ropes used to create a larger or smaller bed.

9.3: Pet Toy Tug Rope

Supplies

- 3 strands of 1/4-inch cotton rope, each measuring 90cm long

- Scissors

- Tape measure

- Tape

Instructions

- Start by measuring and cutting three strands of cotton rope, each measuring 90cm long.

- Gather the three strands of rope and tie a knot at one end, securing them together.

- Divide the strands into three sections, with one strand in each section.

- Start braiding the strands together by crossing the right strand over the center strand, then crossing the left strand over the new center strand.

- Continue braiding in this manner, alternating sides and crossing the outer strands over the center strand.

- As you braid, make sure to keep the tension even and the braids tight. Continue braiding until you reach the end of the strands, leaving a small length at the end.

- Tie a knot at the end of the braided rope, securing all the strands together.

- Trim any excess rope if desired.

- Your pet toy tug rope is now ready for playtime with your furry friend!

9.4: Pet Waste Bag Holder

Supplies

- 1-inch cotton webbing, 12 inches long

- 1-inch metal D-ring

- Fabric scissors

- Sewing machine or needle and thread

- Velcro or snap button closure

- Pet waste bags

Instructions

- Start by folding the 12-inch cotton webbing in half, creating a loop.

- Position the metal D-ring at the folded end of the webbing, with the ring facing inward.

- Secure the D-ring by sewing a straight stitch or using a needle and thread to sew around the edges of the webbing.

- Measure and mark the desired length for your pet waste bag holder. This will depend on the size of the pet waste bags you will be using.

- Cut the webbing at the marked length, leaving a straight end opposite the folded end.

- Fold over the straight end of the webbing to create a flap. This will serve as the closure for the bag holder.

- Attach Velcro or a snap button to the flap and the body of the bag holder to create a secure closure.

- Sew the Velcro or snap button in place using a sewing machine or needle and thread.

- Test the closure to ensure it securely holds the pet waste bags.

- Your pet waste bag holder is now ready to use. Simply attach it to your pet's leash or belt loop for convenient access to waste bags.

9.5: Small Animal Harness

Supplies

- Soft nylon webbing, 1/2 inch wide and 36 inches long

- Metal D-rings, 2 pieces

- Plastic side-release buckle

- Fabric scissors

- Sewing machine or needle and thread

Instructions

- Start by measuring your small animal's chest circumference. This will determine the length of the harness straps.

- Cut the soft nylon webbing into two equal pieces, each measuring half of the chest circumference plus a few inches for adjustability.

- Fold each piece of webbing in half to create a loop.

- Slide one metal D-ring onto each loop of webbing.

- Position the loops on the back of your small animal, ensuring they are comfortable and secure. Adjust the size of the loops as needed to fit your pet snugly.

- Bring the ends of the webbing through the D-rings and back towards the front of your small animal.

- Attach the plastic side-release buckle to the ends of the webbing, creating an adjustable closure system.

- Sew the webbing ends securely to the plastic buckle using a sewing machine or needle and thread.

- Test the fit of the harness on your small animal, making any necessary adjustments to the strap length for a comfortable and secure fit.

- Your small animal harness is now ready to use. Place it on your pet, adjust the straps, and secure the buckle for a safe and enjoyable outing.

9.6: Pet Bandana

Supplies

- Fabric of your choice, approximately 20 inches by 20 inches

- Fabric scissors

- Sewing machine or needle and thread

Instructions

- Start by choosing a fabric that is suitable for your pet's comfort and style. You can select a patterned fabric or a solid color, depending on your preference.

- Measure and cut the fabric into a square shape, approximately 20 inches by 20 inches.

- Adjust the size if needed based on the size of your pet.

- Fold the fabric square in half diagonally to form a triangle, with the right sides of the fabric facing each other.

- Using a sewing machine or needle and thread, sew along the two open edges of the triangle, leaving one edge open for turning the fabric right side out.

- Carefully turn the fabric right side out through the open edge, ensuring the corners are fully turned out.

- Press the bandana flat with an iron, making sure the seams are neatly pressed.

- To create the bandana shape, fold the top corner of the triangle down towards the center, creating a straight edge at the top.

- Fold the bottom corner of the triangle up towards the center, overlapping the top corner slightly.

- Adjust the folds to achieve the desired bandana shape, ensuring that it will fit comfortably around your pet's neck.

- Once you are satisfied with the shape, press the folds with an iron to hold them in place.

- To secure the bandana around your pet's neck, fold the top edge of the bandana down over the back side, creating a casing for the collar.

- Insert your pet's collar through the casing, ensuring it is centered and securely in place.

- Adjust the bandana on your pet's neck to achieve the desired look and comfort.

- Your pet bandana is now ready to be worn and admired!

9.7: Pet Toy Basket

Supplies

- Thick cotton rope

- Fabric of your choice for lining (optional)

- Sewing machine or needle and thread (if adding lining)

- Fabric scissors

- Measuring tape or ruler

Instructions

- Start by deciding on the size of your pet toy basket. Measure and cut the thick cotton rope to your desired length. The length will depend on the size of the basket you want to create.

- Begin shaping the basket by coiling the rope into a tight spiral. Hold the end of the rope and start wrapping it around itself, creating a circular shape.

- Continue coiling the rope, making sure to keep the coils tight and close together. As you coil, use your hands to shape the sides of the basket, gradually building the desired height.

- To secure the rope coils, you can use a hot glue gun to apply a small amount of glue between the layers of rope. Be careful not to burn yourself while working with the hot glue.

- If you prefer a lined basket, measure and cut a piece of fabric that matches the size of the basket's interior. The fabric can be a plain color or patterned, depending on your preference.

- Using a sewing machine or needle and thread, sew the fabric into a cylindrical shape, leaving one end open.

- Slide the fabric lining into the rope basket, ensuring it fits snugly inside. Fold the fabric over the top edge of the basket to create a neat finish.

- If desired, you can secure the fabric lining to the rope basket by hand-stitching it in place or using small dots of hot glue along the top edge.

- Once the lining is in place, you can further embellish the basket by adding decorative elements such as ribbons, bows, or personalized tags.

- Your pet toy basket is now ready to be filled with your furry friend's favorite toys. Place it in a convenient location where your pet can easily access their toys and keep them organized.

9.8: Pet Hammock

Supplies

- 100 feet of sturdy macramé cord or rope

- Wooden dowels or PVC pipes (size and length will depend on the desired size of the hammock)

- Scissors

- Measuring tape

- S-hooks or carabiner clips

Instructions

- Cut four equal lengths of macramé cord, each measuring the desired length of the hammock plus a few extra feet for knots and hanging.

- Take two of the cords and fold them in half. These will serve as the support cords for the hammock. Attach them to the wooden dowels or PVC pipes by creating a lark's head knot.

- Slide the folded end of the cords through the dowel or pipe, then bring the loose ends through the loop and pull tight.

- Separate the support cords and hang the dowels or pipes horizontally at the desired height using S-hooks or carabiner clips. Make sure they are securely fastened.

- Now, take the remaining two cords and fold each one in half. These will be the working cords for creating the macramé design of the hammock.

- Starting from one side, take one set of working cords and cross them over the support cords, creating an "X" shape. The left cord should be in front of the left support cord, and the right cord in front of the right support cord.

- Take the left working cord and pass it over the left support cord and under the right support cord.

- Take the right working cord and pass it under the right support cord and over the left support cord.

- Pull both working cords tight to create a square knot. Repeat this step to create several square knots, moving from left to right or right to left, depending on your preference.

- Continue creating square knots along the length of the support cords, leaving a small gap between each row of knots.

- Once you have reached the desired length of the hammock, tie a final row of square knots.

- Trim any excess cord, leaving a small tail, and secure the knots with a drop of fabric glue or by melting the ends with a lighter (if using a synthetic cord).

- Hang the hammock by attaching the S-hooks or carabiner clips to the support cords, ensuring they are securely fastened.

- Test the stability and adjust the height as needed to accommodate your pet's weight and size.

9.9: Macramé Pet Leash

Supplies

- Macramé cord (choose a color and thickness suitable for your pet)

- Scissors

- Metal swivel snap hook (size appropriate for your pet)

- Measuring tape

Instructions

- Measure and cut a length of macramé cord for your pet leash. The length will depend on the size of your pet and the desired length of the leash.

  As a general guideline, a standard leash length is around 4 to 6 feet.

- Fold the cord in half and find the midpoint. This will be where you attach the metal swivel snap hook.

- Attach the metal swivel snap hook to the midpoint of the cord by threading the folded end through the hook's opening and pulling the loose ends through the loop created. Tighten the loop securely around the hook.

- Now you will start creating the macramé pattern for the leash. Choose a knot pattern that you like, such as a series of square knots or a spiral knot pattern. You can also incorporate additional decorative knots or beads if desired.

- Begin tying the chosen macramé knots below the swivel snap hook. You can create a loop or handle at the top end of the leash by tying a series of knots or using a specific knot pattern.

- Continue tying the knots along the length of the cord, keeping the pattern consistent. Ensure that the knots are tied tightly and securely to provide strength and durability for the leash.

- Once you reach the desired length for your pet leash, finish it off by tying a secure knot at the end. Trim any excess cord, leaving a small tail for a neat and finished appearance.

- Test the leash's strength and security by gently pulling on it. Make any necessary adjustments or tighten the knots as needed.

- Attach the metal swivel snap hook to your pet's collar or harness, and you're ready to go for a walk with your handmade macramé pet leash.

- Regularly inspect the leash for any signs of wear or damage. If you notice any fraying or weakening of the cord, it's essential to replace the leash to ensure your pet's safety.

- Note: While macramé leashes can be visually appealing, it's crucial to prioritize the safety and comfort of your pet. Make sure the leash is securely attached to your pet's collar or harness and that the materials used are sturdy and appropriate for your pet's size and strength.

9.10: Macramé Pet ID Tag

Supplies

- Macramé cord (choose a color and thickness suitable for your pet)

- Scissors

- Metal pet ID tag

- Small jump ring

- Clear adhesive or glue (optional)

Instructions

- Measure and cut a length of macramé cord for your pet ID tag. The length will depend on the size of the tag and the desired length of the finished macramé design. As a general guideline, a length of 12 to 18 inches should be sufficient.

- Fold the cord in half to find the midpoint. This will be where you attach the metal pet ID tag.

- Attach the metal pet ID tag to the midpoint of the cord by threading the folded end through the hole of the tag and pulling the loose ends through the loop created. Tighten the loop securely around the tag.

- Separate the loose ends of the cord, and you will begin creating the macramé design around the tag. Choose a knot pattern that you like, such as a series of square knots or a spiral knot pattern. You can also incorporate additional decorative knots or beads if desired.

- Start tying the chosen macramé knots below the pet ID tag, working with one cord at a time. Keep the knots tight and close together to create a snug and secure cover for the tag.

- Continue tying the knots around the tag, following your chosen pattern. Make sure to leave enough space for the information on the ID tag to remain visible and legible.

- Once you have covered the entire tag with the macramé design, tie a secure knot at the end to finish it off. Trim any excess cord, leaving a small tail for a neat and finished appearance.

- If desired, you can apply a small amount of clear adhesive or glue to the knots to secure them in place and prevent them from unraveling over time. Be careful not to get any adhesive on the ID tag itself.

- Attach a small jump ring to the hole or loop of the metal pet ID tag. This will provide a secure attachment point for connecting the ID tag to your pet's collar or harness.

- Attach the completed macramé pet ID tag to your pet's collar or harness using the jump ring, ensuring it is securely fastened.

- Double-check that all the information on the ID tag is up to date and legible. If any information needs to be updated or changed, do so before attaching the tag to your pet's collar.

9.11: Macramé Fish Tank Decorations

Supplies

- Macramé cord (choose a color and thickness suitable for your fish tank)

- Scissors

- Fish tank decorations (such as small plastic plants, shells, or aquarium-safe ornaments)

- Suction cups or aquarium-safe adhesive (to attach the macramé decorations to the tank)

Instructions

- Measure and cut several lengths of macramé cord, depending on the desired length and number of decorations. Make sure to leave some extra length for tying knots.

- Decide on the type of macramé knots you want to use for your fish tank decorations. Common knots used in macramé include square knots, half-square knots, and spiral knots. Experiment with different knot combinations to create unique designs.

- Begin by attaching one end of the cord to a suction cup or using aquarium-safe adhesive to secure it to the inside of the fish tank. This will act as the anchor for your macramé decoration.

- Start tying your chosen macramé knots using the cord, incorporating any additional elements like beads or shells if desired. Create patterns and textures by varying the types of knots and the spacing between them.

- Continue tying knots and working your way along the cord until you reach the desired length for your decoration.

- Once you have completed the macramé section, attach the other end of the cord to another suction cup or use aquarium-safe adhesive to secure it to the tank.

- Repeat the process to create additional macramé fish tank decorations, varying the lengths, knots, and designs to add visual interest to your aquarium.

- Carefully place the finished macramé decorations in your fish tank, making sure they are positioned securely and will not harm or disturb the fish or other aquatic life.

- Regularly check and clean the macramé decorations to prevent the accumulation of algae or debris. Gently rinse them in water and use a soft brush if necessary.

- Enjoy the unique and handcrafted macramé fish tank decorations, which will add a touch of creativity and natural beauty to your aquarium.

- Note: Ensure that all materials used in the fish tank decorations are aquarium-safe and will not harm the fish or affect the water quality.

Chapter 10: Macramé and Sustainability

The ability to continue existing and developing without diminishing the natural resources available for use in the future is what is meant by the term "sustainability." Within the past half-century, the craft of macramé has undergone significant development. As a result, one can now purchase macramé bottle holders, hat users, key rings, jewelry, garments, shoes, purses, hammocks, swings, cabinets, plant holders, belts, pet collars, wall decor, and many other items. Items made of Macrame may now be found in every room of the house, including the kitchen, where they are displayed as fruit hammocks like fruit baskets.

10.1: Exploring the Eco-Friendly Aspects of Macramé and Its Contribution to Sustainable Living

Macrame can be made with various materials, but discarded cotton cords are my favorite to work with. The basic component of recycled cotton is pre-consumer cotton, which consists of excess material left over from the production of garments or other cotton materials (such as scraps of clothing), which is then transformed into cotton yarn and string.

Cords from 100% recycled cotton are plastic-free, environmentally friendly, and biodegradable. Other components used to make Macrame present are untreated hardwood rings (for use as natural infant teething rings) or driftwood pieces gathered from the local area (to be used as attractive macrame wall hangings). When working on a macrame project, I frequently prefer to include elements such as wool, yarn, the plant hemp, wooden gemstones, or any other piece of material with a distinctive pattern that one has acquired from my neighborhood OP store. Macrame items manufactured by hand do not need a factory or massive production facilities; rather, all that is required is the two hands of an enthusiastic maker. In contrast to mass-produced presents, handmade presents allow for more room for customization, personalization, and originality. They will also endure longer because they are produced using higher-quality materials, attention, and love when created.

10.2: Using Natural and Recycled Materials to Minimize Environmental Impact

This is up to the individual, but if you are searching for a present that is one of a kind, can be produced to order, is sustainable, environmentally friendly, does not include any plastic, and is as beautiful as it is practical. You may wish to look into macrame products. Supporting a local macrame maker also supports the craft skill practiced by that maker. You are assisting them in keeping Macrame's art form and craft alive and passing on their talents to the subsequent generation. Choosing environmentally friendly items, such as natural Macrame, helps promote ethical and sustainable production, boosts small businesses' growth, and reduces the amount of plastic consumed on our earth.

The advantages of both reducing and reusing waste.

Reduces emissions of greenhouse gases, which are a contributing factor in climate change. Lessens the need to save fresh raw materials, which in turn helps prevent pollution. It Saves energy. Reduces emissions of greenhouse gases, which contribute to the planet's changing climate. Contributes to preserving the natural world for the benefit of future generations. Helps to cut down on the amount of garbage that must either be recycled or disposed of in landfills or incinerators. It enables items to be operated to the maximum capacity they were designed for. It results in cost savings.

10.3: Tips for Repurposing Old Fabrics, Ropes, And Items into Macramé Creations

Making macramé masterpieces from used fabrics, ropes, and other items is an excellent method to decrease waste while giving resources you already have a second chance at being useful. The following are some suggestions that will assist you in reusing these materials and incorporating them into your macrame projects:

To create macramé cords from fabric scraps, cut old clothing, mattress covers, or curtain into strips. Mixing and matching different fabric designs and textures can result in fascinating design combinations. Be sure to pick strong textiles to keep their knots after being tied. Look through your garage, shed or storage area for any old or unused ropes and cords you might have stored there. To use them as cords for macramé, you can either untwist them or cut them into shorter lengths. Your designs could benefit from adding texture and visual appeal if you used a different type of rope, such as nylon, polyester, or sisal. T-shirts with jersey fabric: To make a cord comfortable and stretchy for macramé, cut some old t-shirts and jersey fabric into long, narrow strips. These fabric cords are perfect for the creation of necklaces and bracelets. You can also achieve the desired thickness by braiding or twisting together various strips of fabric.

If you have any old lace-like doilies, you can put them to effective use by adding them to the macramé patterns. You could use them as centerpieces or attach them to your macramé decorations or plant hangers and use them as decorative components there.Belts and straps made of animal or fabric no longer wanted can be made into macramé cords. You can cut them into segments or untie them to make individual strands of the material. They can lend a one-of-a-kind quality to your macramé creations, which is especially useful for accessories such as keychains and bag charms. Beads and buttons Take any pieces of jewelry or clothing that you no longer wear or use and remove any beads or buttons you find there. These can be strung onto the macramé cords you use to build your designs to add visual interest or create focus areas.

Repurposed picture frames or embroidery hoops Search for old frames for photos, embroider hoops, or any other round objects that can be recycled rather than purchasing new frames and hoops for your macramé wall hangings.

After removing any glass or backing, you can use the frame or ring as the foundation for your macramé artwork.

Whether they are made of plastic or metal, items such as old keychains, curtain rings, or bath curtain hooks should not be overlooked. These can be recycled in your macramé compositions to function either as connectors or as aesthetic pieces. You'll disinfect them and find inventive ways to use them.

Repurposing old fabrics, ropes, and items is an excellent way to reduce waste and give new life to materials you already have.

In conclusion, here are some tips for incorporating them into your macramé projects:

- **Fabric scraps:** Cut old clothing, mattress covers, or curtains into strips to create macramé cords. Mixing and matching different fabric designs and textures can result in unique and visually appealing designs.

- **Unused ropes and cords:** Look through your storage areas for any old or unused ropes and cords. Untwist them or cut them into shorter lengths to use as macramé cords. Experimenting with different types of rope, such as nylon, polyester, or sisal, can add texture and interest to your designs.

- **T-shirt and jersey fabric cords:** Cut old t-shirts and jersey fabric into long, narrow strips to create comfortable and stretchy cords for macramé. These cords are perfect for making necklaces and bracelets.

- **Lace-like doilies:** If you have old lace-like doilies, incorporate them into your macramé patterns. Use them as centerpieces or decorative components in your macramé decorations or plant hangers.

- **Repurposed belts and straps:** Transform unwanted belts and fabric straps into macramé cords. Cut them into segments or untie them to create individual strands. These unique materials can add character to accessories like keychains and bag charms.

- **Beads and buttons:** Take beads and buttons from old jewelry or clothing and string them onto your macramé cords. They can add visual interest and create focal points in your designs.

- **Repurposed picture frames or embroidery hoops:** Instead of buying new frames or hoops for your macramé wall hangings, search for old picture frames or embroidery hoops. Remove any glass or backing, and use the frames or hoops as a foundation for your macramé artwork.

- **Recycled items:** Don't overlook items like old keychains, curtain rings, or bath curtain hooks. These can be repurposed in your macramé compositions as connectors or decorative elements. Clean and sanitize them before use, and let your creativity find inventive ways to incorporate them.

- **Repurposed clothing:** Transform old t-shirts, jeans, or fabric scraps into macramé plant hangers, wall hangings, or even tote bags. Cut the fabric into strips or use it as a base for weaving patterns.

- **Upcycled glass jars and bottles:** Use macramé techniques to create decorative coverings for glass jars and bottles. These can be used as candle holders, vases, or storage containers.

- **Recycled metal or plastic materials:** Incorporate recycled metal or plastic materials into your macramé designs. This could include repurposing old wire, metal rings, or plastic beads as decorative elements in your projects.

- **Natural materials from the environment:** Explore your local surroundings for natural materials that can be incorporated into your macramé creations. This could include driftwood, seashells, or feathers, adding a unique touch to your designs.

10.4: Eco-Friendly Macramé Creations

By utilizing recycled materials, upcycled items, and eco-friendly fibers, we can create beautiful and environmentally conscious macramé projects. From plant hangers to accessories, these projects not only add a touch of handmade charm to your space but also contribute to reducing waste and promoting sustainability.

1. Upcycled T-Shirt Yarn Plant Hanger

Supplies

- Recycled t-shirt yarn

- Wooden ring

- Scissors

Instructions

- Cut the recycled t-shirt yarn into long strips.

- Attach the t-shirt yarn to the wooden ring using a lark's head knot.

- Create a series of square knots to form the plant hanger.

- Adjust the length as desired and hang your favorite potted plant from the hanger.

2. Denim Jeans Macramé Bag

Supplies

- Old denim jeans or fabric scraps

- Wooden beads

- Scissors

Instructions

- Cut the denim jeans or fabric scraps into long strips.

- Create a netted macramé bag using square knots, alternating with wooden beads for decoration.

- Customize the size and shape of the bag according to your preference.

- Use the macramé bag as an eco-friendly alternative for carrying your belongings.

3. Driftwood Wall Hanging

Supplies

- Driftwood

- Recycled cotton cord

- Scissors

Instructions

- Attach the recycled cotton cord to the driftwood using lark's head knots.

- Experiment with various macramé knots to create a unique design on the driftwood.

- Add decorative elements like beads or feathers if desired.

- Hang the driftwood wall hanging in your space for a natural and sustainable decor piece.

4. Recycled Coasters

Supplies

- Discarded cardboard or cork

- Recycled cotton cord

- Scissors

Instructions

- Cut the cardboard or cork into circular shapes to serve as the base for the coasters.

- Wrap the recycled cotton cord around the base, using square knots or other macramé knots.

- Continue knotting until the coaster is fully covered with the cord.

- Create a set of coasters to protect your surfaces while adding an eco-friendly touch to your home.

5. Upcycled Jewelry with Macramé

Supplies

- Upcycled beads from old jewelry

- Recycled cotton cord

- Scissors

Instructions

- String the upcycled beads onto the recycled cotton cord.

- Use macramé knots such as square knots, half-square knots, or spiral knots to create bracelets, necklaces, or earrings.

- Get creative with different knot patterns and bead arrangements to design unique pieces of eco-friendly jewelry.

- Wear your upcycled macramé jewelry with pride, knowing that you've given new life to forgotten treasures.

6. Recycled Plastic Bag Tote

Supplies

- Recycled plastic bags (cleaned and dried)

- Scissors

- Macramé cord or yarn

- Tape measure

- Large-eye needle

- Closure (e.g., button, magnetic snap, Velcro

Instructions

- Flatten and smooth out the plastic bags. Cut off the handles and bottom seam of each bag.

- Fold one bag in half lengthwise and cut it into long strips, about 1 inch wide. Repeat with the remaining bags.

- Take three plastic strips and tie a knot at one end to secure them together.

- Start braiding the strips, alternating the outer strips over the center strip until you reach the desired length for your tote bag. Tie a knot at the end to secure the braid.

- Cut two long pieces of macramé cord or yarn for the handles. Fold each piece in half and attach them to the top edges of the bag using the large-eye needle. Tie knots to secure the handles.

- To close the tote bag, sew on a button, attach a magnetic snap, or use Velcro as a closure option.

7. Upcycled Glass Jar Hanging Lantern

Supplies

- Clean glass jar with lid

- Macramé cord or string

- Scissors

- Tea light candle

Instructions

- Measure the circumference of the jar's mouth and cut a piece of macramé cord or string to that length.

- Tie a loop knot at one end of the cord and secure it to the lid of the glass jar.

- Start wrapping the cord tightly around the jar from the top, leaving a small gap between each wrap. Continue until you reach the bottom of the jar.

- Tie a knot at the bottom to secure the wrapping.

- Cut another piece of cord and attach it to the sides of the jar, creating a handle for hanging.

- Place a tea light candle inside the jar and screw on the lid. Hang the lantern in a safe and secure location, away from flammable materials.

8. Repurposed Leather Keychain

Supplies

- Leather scraps or old leather belts

- Scissors

- Keychain ring

- Hole punch or leather punch

Instructions

- Cut a piece of leather into a desired shape for your keychain, such as a rectangle or circle.

- Use a hole punch or leather punch to create a hole at the top of the leather piece.

- Insert the keychain ring through the hole.

- Optional: Decorate the leather piece by stamping or painting designs onto it. Attach your keys to the keychain ring.

9. Recycled Paper Macramé Ornaments

Supplies

- Recycled paper (e.g., magazine pages, newspaper)

- Scissors

- Macramé cord or string

- Glue

- Optional: beads, charms, or decorative elements

Instructions

- Cut the recycled paper into long strips, about 1 inch wide.

- Take one strip and fold it in half. Tie a knot at the folded end, leaving a loop for hanging.

- Separate the strip into two halves and fold each half in half again. Tie a knot at the folded ends, creating two smaller loops.

- Repeat steps 2 and 3 with additional paper strips, alternating the colors or patterns for a more decorative effect.

- Arrange the knotted paper strips in a desired pattern, layering and twisting them as you like.

- Cut a piece of macramé cord or string and tie it around the top of the paper strips to secure them together.

- Optional: Add beads, charms, or other decorative elements to the ends of the macramé cord for extra embellishment.

- Hang the macramé ornament in your desired location.

10. Reclaimed Wood Macramé Shelf

Supplies

- Reclaimed wood plank

- Macramé cord or rope

- Drill

- Screws

- Scissors

Instructions

- Measure and mark the desired height for your macramé shelf on the reclaimed wood plank.

- Using a drill, create two holes at the marked spots to attach the macramé cords.

- Cut four equal-length pieces of macramé cord or rope, ensuring they are long enough to reach the desired height and width of the shelf.

- Thread each piece of cord through the holes in the wood plank, leaving equal lengths hanging on both sides.

- Tie knots at the ends of each cord to secure them to the wood plank.

- Gather the four cords together and tie a large knot at the top, creating a loop for hanging the shelf.

- Optional: Add additional knots or macramé embellishments to the hanging cords for decoration.

- Hang the reclaimed wood macramé shelf in your desired location and display your favorite items on it.

Chapter 11: Macramé Business and Selling Crafts

It is usually an excellent plan to practice functioning your Macrame company by selling trivial things to relatives and close friends before you launch your online shop. This will give you a fair sense of what to expect once your online store runs. The more you practice with the individuals you already know, the more comfortable you will grow with pricing your things appropriately, and the better you will become at managing your costs and time spent creating.

11.1: Tips for Starting a Macramé Business or Selling Crafts Online

Do you find it enjoyable to produce tutorials and show other people how they can recreate your work? Then you should look into beginning your channel on YouTube and giving it a shot. Using your skills in Macrame to generate money on YouTube presents an incredible opportunity. Over the years, I've had the pleasure of collaborating with many skilled macrame instructors, and I couldn't be happier to watch their YouTube channels reach more than 100,000 subscribers. Making a video on YouTube doesn't require a high-end camera or any special audio gear. Grab your smartphone, set it up on a tripod, and record yourself putting together DIY projects.

There are several things that, if you do them, will help your YouTube channel expand more quickly. Make sure the video is under 15 minutes in length. Canva allows you to create an attractive and organized thumbnail for your YouTube videos.

You should edit the text to cover the most significant aspects of the knotting procedure rather than the full process. Make sure the title of your video includes the appropriate keywords. Please complete the description and be sure you utilize the appropriate tags. Spread your video around everywhere you can. Do you specialize in education, and are you skilled with a camera? Then why not try creating an online Macramé course that you can sell on sites like Skill Share? No applications or permissions are required, and you are free to work at your speed to have your class ready to post on Skill share whenever you feel ready. If you have much to share about Macrame, you should consider starting a blog.

There aren't many blogs centered on Macrame, but doing so is a fantastic way to share your expertise with others. You can monetize your blog with sufficient traffic by placing advertisements and making money through affiliate marketing by promoting things that readers may be interested in purchasing. You may sell your handcrafted macrame pieces online in many ways. You can leverage your existing social media platforms, such as TikTok, Facebook, and Instagram, to sell your wares online.

Other options include opening a shop on a platform such as Shopify or Squarespace, becoming a member of a marketplace like Etsy or Big Cartel, and so on. Make sure you are aware of any fees a platform may impose for sales before you launch your shop, and factor in these additional costs when determining the prices of your products. You don't necessarily have to sell your pieces; another option is to teach others how to duplicate them. Because it requires less effort and time, selling a pattern as part of your macramé business can effectively generate revenue. Once a design is displayed in your shop, all that remains for you to do is concentrate on selling it.

To sum up, here are some valuable tips to consider:

- **Start small:** Before launching your online shop, practice selling your macramé items to friends and family. This will help you gain valuable experience in pricing, managing costs, and time management.

- **YouTube tutorials:** Consider starting a YouTube channel dedicated to macramé. Share your knowledge and techniques through video tutorials, showcasing your skills and providing step-by-step instructions for creating macramé projects. Building a presence on YouTube can help you reach a wider audience and monetize your channel through advertising and sponsorships.

- **Online courses:** Develop online macramé courses that cater to different skill levels, from beginners to advanced. Platforms like Skillshare and Udemy provide opportunities to share your expertise and earn income from course enrollments.

- **Macramé blog:** Start a blog where you can share your macramé journey, tutorials, and inspiration. Write engaging articles that provide valuable insights and tips for macramé enthusiasts. Monetize your blog through affiliate marketing, sponsored content, and advertising.

- **Online selling platforms:** Utilize popular online platforms like Etsy, Shopify, or Big Cartel to set up your online shop. These platforms provide a ready-made customer base and offer various tools to manage your inventory, process orders, and track sales. Optimize your product listings with high-quality images and detailed descriptions to attract potential buyers.

11.2: Marketing Strategies and Platforms for Promoting Your Macramé Creations

Announce all the social networking sites where you create items and sell them. Don't hesitate to show off images of your new interest at work or on social occasions. Invite friends for a lovely lunch and exhibit your Macrame across the house. TIP: Many individuals will ask you to manufacture goods for them that are beyond the skill level of a beginner because they know you can handle the challenge.

Be sure to teach yourself how to politely decline participation in initiatives you are not interested in working on. Participate in the local Craft Fairs with your Macramé Objects to Sell. It will be a lot of fun for you to set up your very own macrame booth, and it will also help you interact with new consumers.

Establish yourself as a local wholesaler. I wondered if any adorable local boho boutiques or flower and plant shops were in the neighborhood. Show them what you're capable of by approaching them with a modest choice of your best little macramé pieces and demonstrating your skills.

To effectively promote your macramé creations and grow your business, consider the following strategies:

- **Social media presence:** Establish a strong presence on social media platforms such as Instagram, Facebook, and Pinterest. Share captivating images and videos of your macramé creations, engage with your audience, and use relevant hashtags to expand your reach.

- **Collaborations:** Seek opportunities to collaborate with influencers, local businesses, or other artisans in complementary niches. Collaborations can help you reach new audiences and create mutually beneficial partnerships.

- **Craft fairs and markets:** Participate in local craft fairs, markets, and pop-up events to showcase your macramé creations in person. Create an attractive booth display that highlights your unique style and craftsmanship.

- **Personalized commissions:** Offer custom macramé pieces tailored to individual preferences. Emphasize your ability to create unique and personalized designs that resonate with customers. Promote this service through your website and social media platforms.

- **Email marketing:** Build an email list of interested customers and macramé enthusiasts. Send regular newsletters to share updates, new product releases, and exclusive discounts. Provide valuable content and engage with your audience to build trust and loyalty.

- **Local partnerships:** Collaborate with local businesses, such as home decor stores or boutique shops, to showcase and sell your macramé creations. This can help you reach a targeted audience and establish yourself as a trusted local artisan.

- **Packaging and branding:** Pay attention to the presentation of your macramé creations. Invest in quality packaging materials that align with your brand aesthetic. Include personalized thank-you notes or small tokens of appreciation to leave a lasting impression on your customers.

- **Photography and product imagery:** High-quality product images are essential for attracting customers online. Invest in good lighting and staging to capture the beauty and detail of your macramé pieces. Consider hiring a professional photographer or learning photography skills to showcase your creations effectively.

- **Customer engagement and feedback:** Foster strong relationships with your customers by providing exceptional customer service. Respond promptly to inquiries, address concerns, and go the extra mile to ensure customer satisfaction. Encourage customers to leave reviews and testimonials to build trust and credibility.

- **Continuous learning and innovation:** Stay updated with the latest macramé trends, techniques, and designs. Attend workshops, join macramé communities, and seek inspiration from other artists. Experiment with new materials, color palettes, and styles to keep your offerings fresh and appealing to customers.

- **Pricing and profitability:** Determine pricing that reflects the value of your craftsmanship, materials, and time invested. Consider factors such as material costs, labor hours, and overhead expenses when setting your prices.

  Regularly review and adjust your pricing to ensure profitability and sustainability for your business.

- **Shipping and fulfillment:** Develop efficient shipping and fulfillment processes to ensure smooth order processing and timely delivery. Research different shipping carriers and options to find the most cost-effective and reliable solutions. Provide tracking information to customers and communicate any delays or issues promptly.

- **Networking and collaborations:** Connect with other macramé artists, makers, and craft enthusiasts through social media groups, forums, and local events. Collaboration can lead to new opportunities, shared resources, and cross-promotion, expanding your reach and customer base.

- **Continuous improvement:** Strive for continuous improvement in your craft, business operations, and customer experience. Seek feedback from customers, analyze market trends, and adapt your strategies accordingly. Embrace innovation and embrace new technologies and tools that can streamline your business processes.

Remember, success in the macramé business requires a combination of creativity, passion, and strategic planning. Continuously improve your craft, adapt to market trends, and nurture relationships with your customers. With dedication and perseverance, your macramé business can flourish and bring joy to both you and your customers.

Conclusion

Finally, "Macrame for Beginners" has given you the information, skills, and motivation you need to explore the fascinating world of Macrame. You have studied the fundamental knots covered in this book, understood the variety and history of Macrame, and made your projects. However, this is only the start of your macrame journey. You are now prepared to explore and experiment with more complex techniques, projects, and designs because the groundwork has been built. Let your creativity soar as you stretch the Macrame's limits and realize your vision using knots and cords. Remember that Macrame is a form of self-expression and a way to integrate your individuality and flair into each product, not just gorgeous things. Accept the chance to give your Macrame projects a delicate touch by selecting colors, adding beads, or using additional materials. Don't be afraid to venture beyond your comfort zone and take on more challenging designs as you continue practicing and honing your abilities. To create one-of-a-kind works, look for inspiration from other macrame artists, experiment with different knot combinations, and use your imagination. Don't forget about Macrame's therapeutic advantages as well. Spend some time getting lost in the rhythmic flow of the knotting, letting it calm and center you. Macrame can help with mindfulness and provide a peaceful outlet in today's hectic society.

Finally, keep in mind that learning is a lifelong process. As your macrame skills improve, keep looking for added resources, becoming involved in communities, and going to workshops or classes to broaden your knowledge and meet other lovers. The macrame community is active, encouraging, and willing to exchange knowledge and skills.

You've started a creative and joyful adventure with "Macrame for Beginners" as your guide. Accept the pleasure of knotting, let your creativity soar, and watch as your macrame creations develop and astound you. The options are unlimited, whether you make macrame items for yourself, close friends, or even as a prospective business idea.

We escalate you were joining us on this amazing journey. May your macrame journey be full of beauty, inspiration, and fulfillment; may your knots be tight and your creativity limitless. Happy tying!

Printed in Great Britain
by Amazon

29895360R00068